MW01106890

BETWEEN THE MERIDIANS

BETWEEN THE MERIDIANS

JIM CHRISTY

Ekstasis  Editions

Canadian Cataloguing in Publication Data

Christy, Jim
    Between the Meridians

    ISBN 1-896860-60-5

    1. Christy, Jim, 1945- --Journeys. 2. Voyages and travels. I. Title.
    G465.C57 1999   910.4'.54   C99-911054-3

© Jim Christy, 1999.
Cover and text photographs: Jim Christy
Author photo: James Eke.

Acknowledgements
Some of these stories and travel pieces have appeared in the following
magazines: *Weekend Magazine, Western Living Magazine, 'V'
magazine, Kelowna Courier, Equity, The Georgia Straight, Quest.*
    Many of stories in the book have never been published before

Published in 1999 by:
Ekstasis Editions Canada Ltd.   Ekstasis Editions
Box 8474, Main Postal Outlet   Box 571
Victoria, B.C. V8W 3S1   Banff, Alberta T0L 0C0

THE CANADA COUNCIL | LE CONSEIL DES ARTS
FOR THE ARTS | DU CANADA
SINCE 1957 | DEPUIS 1957

Between the Meridians has been published with the assistance of a grant from the
Canada Council and the Cultural Services Branch of British Columbia.

For
Kevin Brown
and
Joe Ferone

The elsewhere is here in the immediacy of real life. It is from here that our thoughts rise up, and it is here that they must come back. But after what travels! Live first, then turn to philosophy; but then in the third place, live again.

Rene Daumal

Make the universe your companion.

Basho

Let's get the damned show on the road.

Angelo Christinzio

Contents

ROADS

But above all there was the running burglar, a huge pack on his back
On the road whitened by the moon
Escorted by the barking of dogs in the sleeping villages
And by the cackle of the hens suddenly awakened.
I'm not rich, says the phantom, shaking the ashes off his cigar,
                                                    I'm not rich
But I'll bet a hundred dollars that he'll go far if he continues.
Vanity, all is vanity, answered the crow.

Robert Desnos

SPELL ON ME

Y ou what?" Hardly believing her ears but wanting to believe her ears, my mother proceeded cautiously, afraid of a trick.

"Yeah, I do. I wanna go."

"You want to go on your class trip?"

"Yeah, Ma. Annapolis, Maryland."

"They're taking your class to the Naval Academy at Annapolis and you want to go?"

"Uh huh. I've always been interested in ships and stuff."

"Well, I'm just a little, well, surprised. But if I thought you meant it and you promised not to cause trouble, I'd sign this form so you could go."

She had every right to be surprised. The school started you out on these trips in your freshman year. You were taken some place in the fall and to some other place in the late spring. Here it was May of my sophomore year and I had missed all three trips of my high school career. Quite frankly, my grades had been too low for that first one mainly because I didn't apply myself. I was bored. You had to qualify, it being an honour and a privilege to travel to, for instance, Washington, D.C., a journey designed to fill you with pride and patriotism as you embarked on the great adventure of high school.

The second was to Gettysburg and the battlefield. It was bad enough having to put up with all those kids at school without being around them on an outing, was the way I looked at it. We didn't have to go to war on that because my mother, being a genuine southern lady or "an unreconstructed rebel" as the old man described her, didn't have any love for Gettysburg and all that it signified. Ah, but the great historical sites of Philadelphia were another matter.

The birthplace of the nation. Had I no respect for my country? They don't have such shrines as the Liberty Bell and Independence Hall in Russia, Mr. Smarty Pants.

In the end, I simply refused to hand in the paper which she had filled out.

But I was hot to go to Annapolis. I hadn't been seized by patriotism, nor had my orientation done an about face. Being a cadet was my idea of nothing to do. Now, getting on a ship and sailing to exotic ports certainly had a strong appeal but if I did that I bet I'd be wielding a shovel and choking on smoke down in the engine room. Not for me to step proudly ashore in Singapore or Surabaya in one of those goofy uniforms looking for a dark-skinned hooker about whom I could make allusions thirty years later in the company of my fellow Elks or Lions—looking but probably not hiring for fear of some terrible disease such as one always contracted in those kinds of places from people who had no idea of hygiene—(they'd shown movies on board)—so I'd sit in Texas Pete's drinking good old Pabst Blue Ribbon beer, calling the little waiter Amigo and talking about the World Series with a guy who kept trying to sell me his sisters until the Second Looey punched him in the mouth, precipitating a full-scale Hey Rube!—and I'd escape with an ashtray.

Later for that, dad. Annapolis was the home of WEXI, the radio station that I listened to at night in my room while supposedly doing homework. No top forty station that; no surf music on WEXI; neither was there Motown. No, sexy WEXI was rhythm and blues with the emphasis on the rhythm. You could only get it in the evenings in my town of Brookdale. Roy Brown, Wynonie Harris, Screamin Jay Hawkins, Little Eva, the Orioles, and the fellow the record spinners referred to as "the world's hippest white man"—Johnny Otis. All those solid sounds. I'd sit with a dreary textbook in front of me, desk drawer open, finger on a little transistor in there, listening, and listening also for the counterpoint squeak that meant my mother was sneaking up the stairs to catch me at anything other than serious study. I was ready to flick the switch, close the drawer and frown in concentration over Tennyson and the isosceles triangle.

And all the time, I'm dreaming as the music came floating across the Chesapeake Bay, up Highway Forty, the truck route, overtop miles of suburban rooftops, and right into my window. It put a spell on me.

So, naturally, even if it meant getting a haircut—and it did—I was going to take that class trip to Annapolis. Even if I had to wear the checkered sports jacket and tie—and I did—and pile into the school bus with guys who sincerely thought it would be wonderful to attend the Naval Academy—those who weren't leaning toward West Point or the lowly Air Force place out in Colorado—and with girls who giggled at the prospect of seeing all those cute future officers.

And there we were on Friday morning, early enough that our breath made little puffs in the air, most of the sophomore class gathered around two yellow buses. I noticed some of the girls had applied a touch of pancake makeup. Several of the big shot athletes were striking attitudes, practicing to impress the coaches at Navy.

It took only a couple of hours to get to Annapolis and, not surprisingly, I had a seat to myself. Staring out the window I tried to ignore the antics of my classmates who bopped each other on the head, let go the usual sounds of flatulence and made fun out loud of those below them in the hierarchy. And no one was lower in the hierarchy than me. All of that visible in the window around the corona of my own dumb haircut.

We disembarked at the Naval Academy where sunshine glinted off rooftops and tradition was the mortar that held in place colonial stone. Young men in uniform marched purposefully over swards of green. We were met by a middle-aged moron with a head like the business end of a clothesbrush who was to be our tour guide. Immediately he began barking out instruction and information, his whole bearing and attitude a reminder of what us guys could expect if we should by any chance—slim as it might be—measure up to the rigorous standards of the Naval Academy.

"We'd make men out of you here," he threatened, and now and again favoured the girls with a remark which, though invariably condescending, nevertheless elicited fits of happy giggling.

We saw a typical lecture hall where swabbies took notes while a man who looked just like them only older tapped at a blackboard with a pointer and indicated where to deploy the aircraft carrier and where the trusty old dreadnaught.

We walked hallowed halls and through a museum and finally wound up at the football stadium where the guide spoke reverently of the great Navy teams of bygone years and of fabled tourneys with Army at Franklin Field in Philadelphia. Some of Brookdale's own gridiron worthies took all this in with solemn respectful expressions, others were merely obsequious.

The mess hall was evidently a sacred place so we missed the opportunity to watch midshipmen attack their chow, or gobs filling their gobs, as I remarked to the kid next to me in line whose name was Wissledome. He gave me a dirty look.

We were bussed into the quaint little burg and led to the banquet room of a restaurant on Main Street where a pair of harassed waitresses served chicken a la king. The walls were festooned by watercolours of sailboats and the large shield of the Lion's Club. Some of the athletes threw dinner buns at the nerds. Later that afternoon we were to return to the Naval Academy to hear a lecture delivered to the entire student body on the Navy's role in providing a bulwark against the communist menace. But immediately after lunch, the agenda called for a constitutional along the harbour for the purpose of viewing the very boats represented by the restaurant watercolours. That to be followed by a turn around the historical society. I never made any of it.

Quite pleased was I to be out on the streets of Annapolis even if I was trudging in lock-step. I supposed that the negroes here would have a different air about them, that the very air itself would be imbued with reminders of the music I listened to in secret. Maybe the wispy clouds would form themselves into half-notes, the breeze carry a tender alto refrain that only the hip and the trees could hear, and all'd swing accordingly.

The lady there. Does she know Esther Phillips personally? That cat hopping off the back of the newspaper truck with wire-wrapped bundles in his hands? Why's he frowning? Put in mind of cotton bales? His baby run out taking the Lincoln? Those tears? Don't wipe them away—they're souvenirs in disguise—of a love gone astray.

On the pleasant afternoon streets of Annapolis, I was doing manic head rotations on the lookout for a sign, any sign, I could interpret to my liking. To the right was Ye Olde Card and Gift Shoppe, a reminder in the window that Mother's Day was fast approaching—nothing there. To the left: parked cars, moving traffic, a baggy-brown suit, a parking meter, a telephone pole. But, wait. There was a scrap of yellow, the edge of a yellow sign stapled to the telephone pole and down in the corner of that, a small photo of a man with dark skin and pomaded hair. I reined in, causing Wissledome in back of me to tred on my heel, and retreated for a closer look.

On the poster were photos of other dark-skinned people. They were not the newly appointed faculty members of the Northern Negro Normal School. They were Bobby Bland, three women and two men in evening dress called The Ebonylites, and the one and only

Screamin Jay Hawkins.

They were the attractions at a dance sponsored by none other than good old WEXI. And the dance was this very night.

Hey now! Well now!

I hustled back in line, my mind racing like three honking tenors at a cutting session in the back room of the Royal Roost.

Our bus was to leave for Brookdale at five, the show started at eight. If I disappeared from the crowd and stayed over, it would cause trouble, a lot of trouble. First of all, the chaperones would feel it incumbent upon themselves to spend at least fifteen minutes searching for me. Maybe notify the cops that there was a lost student. The dance probably wouldn't be over until midnight and, of course, I'd have to find a place to stay until morning. I had six dollars in my pocket. Naturally, they'd suspend me from school for the standard three days and that would mean three points off each grade per day, and I didn't exactly have points to spare. Then there was the hassle on the homefront. My mother would go on the rampage, suspend all privileges—such as they were—double the chores and, worst of all, keep referring to the incidents for months. All that versus the chance to see Jay Hawkins, Bobby Blue Bland and the Ebonylites, whoever they were. I considered both sides of issue and made my decision. It took about a New York minute.

"What the hell you so excited for, Christy?"

This from Wissledome who was a big fellow with a little haircut and a large attitude on account of he'd made the junior varsity baseball team.

"Uh, I gotta piss, Wissledome."

"Christ, Christy, your either off somewhere saying nothing to nobody or you're jumping around like a nigger with the runs."

"Yeah, and you Wissledome. You're the only guy I ever seen'd have to grow his hair out to get into the Naval Academy."

Up ahead the street ended at a pocket-sized park with the usual statue at the centre. There was a gas station on one corner and a museum on the other.

"Hey, Wissledome. Anybody asks, I've gone over there to the station to take a piss."

"Yeah, don't pull on it too much."

"Why not? You ought to try it, day you locate yours."

The sophomore class made a squad's right and I made a squad's left all by myself, and kept on going.

I hid out in various diners until show time.

Embarrassed? Well I should say so. It was bad enough having to be inside that sports jacket with the maroon and brown checks separated by a tasteful tope grid pattern around Brookdale where it was considered the apex of Junior Jaycee fashion—but to wear it at an affair such as this—me knowing that I was sort of an ofay parody —was the limit of humiliation. The only thing missing was the plastic thing on my breast pocket that announced, "Hi, I'm the third annual winner of the young Art Linkletter lookalike contest."

The two young ladies at the card table with their coils of tickets did not laugh at me but did exchange the kind of look whose purpose was mutual wordless assurance that their eyes did not deceive. I passed on bravely into the hall where things were already jumping. Couples danced to records and, rather than hide in a corner, I took a bold turn around the big room to display myself, for better or worse. Most ignored me; the ones who checked me out did so without apparent hostility.

I was not the only white person present, merely the sole white male. There were half a dozen white women, five of them blondes. They were with, or in the vicinity of, their men. You'd see two blondes at a table talking and glancing over to where their gentlemen were standing with others taking care of pressing business.

After Bullmoose Jackson was done singing about his Big Ten Inch (Record That Plays the Blues), the lights dimmed, chairs scraped and talk subsided. A fat man in a white suit and brown-and-white shoes came out on stage and told some filthy jokes. After the crowd was warm, he introduced, "The Man...Mister....Bobby...Blue Bland!"—who strolled out, real cool, in an electric blue sharkskin suit, sporting a high pomaded pompadour. His combo followed, slowly heeling and toeing, four guys who looked like they were out on a day pass from Maximum Security. Then came a girl in a silvery dress, cut way down to there and slit way up to here, to strap Mr. B. into his guitar. As the young lady walked off, Bobby Blue Bland gestured toward her with his instrument, the crowd responded raucously, and he launched into a set that was to last without a pause for forty-five minutes.

Two songs in, sweat had turned electric blue to indigo. Four songs in, I was emboldened to ask a girl to dance. "Certainly," she replied, and the number of girls I'd danced with during my high school career immediately doubled.

It was a novelty for her as well so she danced with me another time before passing me on to her friends. The third young lady allowed as how it was kind of strange me being there and all, and I said, "Well, yeah. I'd been looking for the Frankie Avalon sockhop and some silly joker directed me here."

After a fifteen minute intermission, the Ebonylites appeared. They were an a capella group in satin gowns and tuxedos. They did their entire smooth set in front of the curtains within a big buttery moon of a spotlight. When they finished, the spot followed them off and was extinguished.

The stage remained dark. You heard the creaking of pulleys as curtains were drawn back. A pinpoint of light hit the stage, widening gradually. There was what looked to be a long rectangular crate, rounded on top and set on a pair of sawhorses. Light shone on the polished surface and glinted off a metal rail along the side of the crate.

"Hey, man! That's a coffin!," someone called out. "And they's flowers around it. What the hell!"

And as the light continued to expand, you saw six ladderback chairs, three on each side of the coffin. Four of the chairs were occupied by men with glum expressions, hands folded in their laps; the other two chairs held full-grown skeletons, fingers entwined on boney laps.

Four skulls rested on the floor, and pink and lavender smoke began to ooze from their orifices. It was like the stage hands had made a drastic mistake and removed the wall separating the theatre and a weird funeral home next door.

There was a grating metal sound like the big rusty door to the castle dungeon being opened by a Carpathian hunchback. The coffin lid rose. A dead man was inside, you could barely make him out: tips of pointy shoes, hands at peace over his stomach, the caulked prow of his 'do, everything nestled in pink satin.

More than a few voices gasped when the man in the coffin raised his head. Then he was sitting all the way up, and we could get a load of his lamé tuxedo, which matched the coffin lining. A lone baritone voice in the crowd called "Shee-it!"

The dead man opened his eyes wide, looked straight ahead in mock fright, and screamed, "I I I I Eeeehhh Aaaahhh Eaaayaah!"

While he emitted this strangled, tortured cry, the four gentlemen mourners bent and released upon the floor, four sets of large white teeth that proceeded to travel across the stage, chattering as they went. Some of the men reached under their chairs, produced guitars or saxophones and walked, grim as pallbearers to their positions, while the man in the coffin continued to wail: "I I I I Eeeehhh Aaaahhh Eaaayaah!"

The black drapes behind him parted, revealing the drummer and his kit. Partially revealed, that is, because the drummer wore shades, his suit was black, his shirt black, tie black and he was black. There was, however, a pink phosphorescent skull-and-crossbones painted on his bass drum. The points of his sticks glowed the same pink.

"IIIEEEEEHHHAAAAAAHHHAAAAAYAAH!"

The dead man climbed down from his eternal resting place.

The drummer responded with a riff of snare and tom tom and ended on a rim shot. From each wing of the stage appeared a fat woman carrying a pink spear. Adorned in nothing save grass skirts and pasties, they barefooted it toward the coffin. The women had bones through their wigs and pink hoops through noses and ears. They tipped the coffin forward before hustling off stage shaking all over as berserk sets of teeth chased after them.

"Ahhh Ahhh Ahhh.....Put a spell on you!" cried the man in pink, stepping forward robotically as the crowd stomped and called out in response. But Screamin Jay appeared oblivious to the commotion and did the entire song while presuming to be in a zombie trance.

He snapped out of the spell for the next number, a hard driving R and B mumbo jumbo nonsense compendium, strictly a dog's breakfast of barnyard sounds, pseudo Zulu, ersatz German and vaudeville Chinese with several olés thrown in for good measure. He followed that with a song called Alligator Wine, and jumped around like a prizefighter doing the Mashed Potatoes. Then Screamin Jay strode to the standup mike, began snapping his fingers and started crooning, of all things, *I Love Paris.* This he executed with serious, impeccable phrasing, with melismatic flourishes and a big Billy Eckstine ending: "Be...cause my LOVE is THEEEERRRRRE."

It was his way of letting you know, in case you just might be wondering, that he could sing like a mother, sing with the best of them, if he wished.

He began That Old Black Magic in the same vein, even got halfway through before the skulls began to smoke, the teeth to chatter, and him to start jiving and mocking Frank Sinatra. I pretended not to notice that people looked over at me.

No one had any idea what the man was going to do next. Nonsense or straight ballads, satirizations of standards held dear by the likes of Steve and Edie, and the rest of them, rock and roll, blues, jump, anything, in fact, but the predictable. After an hour, he returned to "I I I Eeeehhh Aaaahhh Eaaaayaaaah!" to the ending of which he added: "UUUhhh...UHHH...UURRRRRHHHH!" which turned out to be the opening to another one of his compositions, Constipation Blues.

This classic ended with everyone shouting, laughing, yelling, applauding, calling out for more. After a lavish bow, Screamin Jay ran through a five minute medley and suddenly the stage went black. A spot hit him and he began to shuffle away, waving over his shoulder like Jimmy Durante. When he got to the coffin, he climbed back in, brought down the coffin lid, and brought down the house.

A wild ovation.

And curtain.

I left the hall and went out into the dark streets of Annapolis. Too excited to sleep, I walked around for an hour then got a room at a negro boarding house.

In the morning, after a breakfast of eggs, grits, side bacon and cornbread, everything sprinkled liberally with Louisiana hot sauce, I hit the road, goosing the ghost toward home and another kind of pandemonium that awaited me there.

WAITING FOR PACO

It's nine thirty in the morning in Oaxaca, my first day back in town. The zocalo and alameda are crowded and the cafes around their perimeter are filled. Things look the same as the last time, and the time before that, and as they always have, probably. The zocalo was already here for the Spanish to orient themselves when they took over in the early 1500's.

Tonight the marimba orchestra will be installed in the leafy bandstand and on Sunday the town orchestra on folding chairs on the afternoon grass will play European classical music. The shoeshine guys are always there kneeling before their green thrones, stealing glances at customers reading *Noticias* or *La Jornada.*

I had just finished my breakfast and ordered another coffee, told a kid I didn't want to buy glass parrots, another one that her necklaces held no allure, and leaned back in the chair when I heard a woman summon her partner's attention with an emphatic: "Hey, look!"

I glanced over just as he was raising his head from a Lonely Planet guidebook.

"That woman over there in the square."

"You mean the zocalo," he corrected her before looking

24

where she indicated.

"Yes, Charles. See her? How she walks?"

"Stiffly."

"Yes, but there's something sort of, I don't know, elegant about her. Regal almost."

I glanced over to where they were looking. For a moment, I didn't recognize her. Then, it was as if my consciousness, which had taken a later plane, finally caught up to me here on the terrace and whacked me on the head, told me to think back nearly two decades to the first of many times I'd seen her.

Only five years ago her hair was still mostly black, her face hadn't gotten its wrinkles and her figure didn't resemble this one. Not that there's anything the matter with her figure now. For an older woman.

She walked toward her usual green wrought iron bench, stopped before it, removed the shawl with a flourish and laid it across the seat.

"You see how she did that," the young woman said. "So proudly, like a bullfighter."

"A matador," said the guy.

Franny sat down and glanced over toward the cathedral and across the alameda to the corner where you'd get off the bus if you were coming from out of town. The corner where a taxi from the airport might drop a visitor. I could imagine her sighing before she reached into her cloth bag and brought out her book.

I turned back to my paper and my coffee but after several minutes, the young woman said, "I've been studying her."

"Who?" her companion asked.

"That woman."

"Why?"

"She interests me."

"Laura, she's just a fifty–something gringo woman, a, uh, gringa."

25

"Every few minutes she looks up from her book and gazes off in the same direction."

"So what's so interesting about that?"

"She doesn't look anywhere else. Isn't curious about what's going on in back of her or in the cafes. Also the kids selling stuff ignore her. She just gazes off into the distance, then down at her book."

"Maybe she's waiting for somebody."

"Yeah, but still..."

"She is waiting for someone," I couldn't help saying over my shoulder.

He didn't exactly give me a hostile look but the fellow was definitely suspicious. The woman raised her eyebrows. They were both in their early thirties with that whitecollar outdoorsy look as if, back in North America, they spent days in offices and their free time on mountain bikes. There were two plastic water jugs on the table.

She was expecting me to say something else.

"And she's been waiting a long time."

"You know her then?" the woman, Laura, asked.

"Oh, yeah."

Charles stared at me.

"How long have you been in Oaxaca?" she asked.

"Just got in last night."

"Well" he said, "how could you know what's going on?"

He pressed his lips together as if he was stopping me in my tracks before I could put one over on them. There was probably a warning in the guide book.

The young waiter came to their table and set down two cafe con leches.

"I got in last night but I've been here before, and I first met that woman, Franny Tompkins, many years ago."

She gave him one of those looks such as pass between people who are used to each other but that are inscrutable to others.

"Who's she waiting for?" Laura asked.

"A guy called Paco."

"She been waiting a long time, eh?" Laura said it, and Charles glanced around the terrace with an exasperated expression.

"Yeah, a long time," I answered. "Twenty years."

"What do you mean, twenty years?"

"Just that."

"Well how...? I mean.."

"Look, it's a long story."

"We have time," she said.

"Laura! We're supposed to go to the museum," he said and started to get up, "The Rufino Tamayo Museum."

"That can wait, Charles."

He sat back down.

"Well?" she said.

"Well it was back in 1979, in February, early February. Hell, twenty years ago almost to the day. Reason I know is, I'd just come from Zihautanejo where I'd been during the Dia de las Candeleras. What we call candlemas. After a week in the city here, I was ready for a walk on the beach. What people often do here at the weekends is ride the bus, or take the plane, over the mountains to Puerto Escondido. Which is what I did and I met Franny Tompkins on the bus headed for the beach. She was with her girlfriend whose name was Neera."

"You remember the name of her friend from twenty years ago?" Charles asked that.

"Yeah, I do."

He smirked, just a little twist at the corners of his mouth but I caught it.

"We only talked a little bit on the bus. Franny and Neera were sitting a couple of seats in front of me and on the other side of the aisle. It was a rough trip back then and it hasn't improved. Seven or eight hours over bad road, Mexico 131. So conversation was difficult.

But I found out they were from Kingston, Ontario, and down in Mexico on a two week holiday.

The next afternoon, walking the sand at Puerto Escondido, beyond the municipal beach on the other side of the rocks, I saw three teenaged boys, none more than fifteen, hanging around a couple of women lying on blankets. Or, rather, I noticed white female legs and now a glimpse of shoulder or elbow. When the kids walked off, I saw Neera and Franny.

"Hey, you're too old for us," Franny called.

They both laughed. They had some beer in a styrofoam cooler. Neera offered me one. When I'd finished it, Franny made a remark about how no boys had stopped by since I'd been sitting there. She tried to pass it off as a joke.

"Well I sure don't want to interfere with your action," I said in the same tone. "I'd look for some girls that same age but I'd get arrested, given the double standard about these sort of things."

A few minutes later, I started back down the sand, thinking about all the middle–class white women who travelled to beach towns like this looking for men. In places like Jamaica and the Bahamas, they could find them; in Mexico, they usually had to settle for boys.

Escondido was a fishing village a long time ago. Its name means hidden port but it had been found by the late Seventies. Still, only a few outsiders braved the bad road back then. The waterfront street had a few restaurants and palapa bars, souvenir shops and a couple of hotels. On Saturday night, I ran into the girls from Kingston who were trying to choose a restaurant. They hadn't tried my favourite so I recommended that for a fish dinner. Franny kept checking her watch. She had a "date" at nine. This one she called a "young man" and not a boy. They'd met the night before.

"His name's Paco. He's eighteen. I took him to bed last night. I haven't been fucked three times in one night since I was in high school."

"Fran–nee!"

28

"I'm sorry if I offended your delicate ears, Neera. But I think I'm in love."

"Oh, give me a break!"

"Is that envy I hear?"

"Hardly. Well...maybe a tiny bit."

We finished dinner, had a drink at another place, and Franny went off to meet her boy. Neera and I walked on the beach. She said it was weird about Franny, how she seemed to be going after young guys with a vengeance. Before this Paco, she already tried out two others in the two days they'd been at Escondido.

They'd known each other since high school. Franny'd married a professor at Queen's University but they divorced a few years ago. During that time she had been in and out of relationships that everyone else could see were doomed from the start. All with the same sort of man.

"They all seemed pale and unhealthy, university types or, well, guys who made you think they spent all their time indoors in basements," Neera explained. "And they probably did."

Around about midnight her hotel hove into view and Neera said, "Well you're not eighteen."

"No," I said. "I'm not. But still I'm younger than you. Let's see..."

"Don't count."

The next day, we ran into Franny and her Paco lying on the beach. He was tall, a good looking guy, acne had left traces on his cheeks and forehead but that saved him from being pretty. Paco was lying on his back, Franny on her right side, her left hand fooling with the Virgin of Guadeloupe medallion on his chest.

"Look at her," Neera muttered. "It's embarrassing."

"This is Paco," she said. It was as if she was introducing Lupita herself. Only Paco was no virgin. What he was was a hustler. He gave me the look, a hustler's instant assessment of whether I was any threat to his game.

"Excuse me, senor."

It was the waiter on the terrace in Oaxaca, in the present time.

I was about to tell him that yes, I would like another coffee but he addressed me in Spanish.

"There was a Paco? You met him? It's true?"

"Yes, there really was a Paco."

The waiter told me that he had been seeing the gringa in the zocalo since he was a little boy but he'd never believed the stories he'd heard. He said he was on his break. He obviously wanted to hear more so I invited him to sit at my table. I translated that exchange for Laura and Charles and continued the tale.

Franny gave Paco some bills to buy four beers and off he went. She talked in a rush, looking after him. "He's had such a tough life. Nine brothers and sisters back in Mexico City; his father died when he was seven; Paco used to be one of those cliff divers in Acapulco. He wants to better himself. I'm going to teach him English and help him emigrate to Canada."

"You better watch yourself, Franny," Neera said.

"You should have told me that about all the others I've been involved with."

"I think I did."

"Paco's not like them. White men are just so dull." She shot me a quick glance, "No offense."

"None taken," I mumbled.

"Franny, it's true all the men I've ever seen you with were white and dull as dishwater but they were also the same type of man."

"Shhh! Here he comes. He's jealous. I like that."

Paco handed around our beers and handed Franny some change, about half of what she was entitled to. Franny didn't notice but Paco saw that I did.

Monday morning I said goodbye to Neera and got on the bus

back to the city.

Two months later, I ran into Franny in Oaxaca at the Bamby bakery. She was at the cash register with a tray of sugary buns. Christina, the Spanish woman who owned the store—and practically the entire block—was holding up three fingers. Franny handed over the coins.

"Paco likes these," she told me.

Behind her, Christina glanced at Franny, looked at me, and twirled her index finger beside her head.

Christina was my landlady.

"I'm going to meet Paco in the Zocalo at ten," Franny said, as we walked out. "We had six glorious weeks together on the beach. But he had to rush back to Mexico City because his mother is gravelly ill. I gave him some money to help her and the children. Actually, he was supposed to be here yesterday but, well, you know how the buses are down here. I hope there wasn't any trouble at home."

I walked to the zocalo with Franny and was going to sit with her for a couple of minutes but she told me I better not.

"If Paco sees you he might be jealous. Especially because it's you. He told me I should stay away from you. So we better only talk when we're sure he's not around."

"Okay, Franny, I get it. Good luck."

I took a seat on the terrace. Ten o'clock came around and no Paco. At noon, Franny got up and walked off. The next day, the same thing. Then I left Oaxaco and didn't make it back for eight years.

That time, I was with my wife. It was after breakfast, and I saw Franny. I recognized her but it was a couple of seconds before it all came back to me. She remembered me too.

Franny told me she'd never returned to Canada. She liked it in Oaxaca where her trust fund went a long way.

"Anyway, I can't leave on account of Paco."

"Paco, yeah. What's he up too?"

She looked at her watch.

"I'll know in about twenty minutes. He's going to meet me here at ten o'clock. Oh, yeah. I remember, you're the one he didn't like, so we better talk later, eh?"

"Sure, Franny."

We walked off.

"What was that all about?" my wife asked.

I told her. I also told the story to my pal Kevin Brown one morning in '94 at about eleven in the morning after I introduced him to Franny Tompkins sitting in the zocalo.

And now I was telling it to these two tourists, Laura and Charles, and to the waiter whose name was Santos.

"She's nuts," Charles said. Laura gave him a disappointed look that turned into one of disgust when he put his hand on the video camera and said, "Should I tape her?"

Santos shook his head sadly. "Viente anos," he said, and got up to go back to work.

I left the terrace and walked over to the zocalo. It was ten minutes to ten and just enough time left to go and say hello to Franny.

JIM CHRISTY

WEST OF KEREMEOS

I've always had secret places in the outdoors, spots with special, private significance, and I feel kind of sorry for people who don't have them. I don't mean recreational or commercial sites or tourist attractions. A secret place may be a waterfall that you can only get to after hiking a day and a half from the end of a logging road but it could also be a neighborhood garden or a hidden shady spot at the back of a field. Wherever it is, it probably serves as a refuge, a place that, perhaps, calls to mind the hideaways of childhood and summons forth an almost atavistic sense of adventure and mystery. It could be anywhere.

A sense of adventure and mystery.

For me it is at the base of a cliff in the Similkameen Valley in southern British Columbia, between Hedley and Keremeos, and I have been going there for many years. I was first lead to the spot by some stories I stumbled upon back in the early Eighties. These told of a conflict between native Indians of the region and Spanish conquistadores, hundreds of years earlier. Supposedly, pictographs existed that "proved" the "truth" of it all.

But these stories were vague and had been written down by white people. I went to the Similkameen, asked questions, poked around for directions and information without much success before being directed to someone who more than a few people insisted would know the truth.

"You must be the guy's been looking for me," said the old man, Ernie Joseph, looking up from the glass of beer he was worrying that late November Saturday afternoon.

"How did you know?"

"Mocassin telegraph. You gonna sit down, or what?"

After I ordered us a couple more, this Indian man who was seventy-eight years old or, at least, that's what he thought he was, told me what I had come to hear. He didn't swear up and down that it was true. He didn't care whether I believed it or not.

"See this is what happened. There were white men who came into this country, along the river there, and there were hundreds of them, many on horseback, and they set up camp not too far from where we're sharing this beer..."

The whites were Spaniards and their camp was near the Indian village of Keremeos. A quarrel ensued between a Spanish soldier and an Indian man. The Indian got the best of the white man who later provoked his compatriots to seek revenge. The Spaniards attacked the native village, taking the people by surprise. They killed many and fled with several prisoners. Their route was up Keremeos Creek, over the hills and across the plains to the foot of Lake Okanagan. The Spaniards followed an old Indian trail along the east side of the lake until they came to a spot north and east of the future site of Kelowna. Here they erected substantial quarters and stayed the winter. The Spaniards were looking for gold but, by spring, having found none and having been subjected to all manner of illnesses, as well as to minor but annoying sniper attacks, they left the area by the same route they had come, eventually returning to Keremeos Creek. Early one morning, while still asleep, the Spaniards were attacked by warriors of the Similkameen tribe, and slaughtered to a man.

After the massacre, the Indians buried the Spaniards

somewhere between their latest campsite and the Keremeos village. This burial place has come to be known as the Spanish mound.

I asked Ernie Joseph when these events had taken place, and he patiently counted forefathers on his fingers before saying with assurance, "Early seventeenth century."

"But according to the history books, the first white man to penetrate the southern interior of what is now called British Columbia was the fur trader David Thompson in 1811. And you said they were on horseback. History books insist horses were unknown even on the coast until the 1750's."

"History books are written by white men. Even if I could read good, I wouldn't believe the half of it."

"Yes, but..."

"Yes, but I got a question for you."

"Okay."

"It's about them horses. You say the history books say our people didn't have horses until the 1750's, and also the books tell there were no white men here until 18–whatever it is. So tell me how did the white men who wrote the history books know when there were horses and other white men if they hadn't got there yet?"

He smiled when I didn't have an answer right away.

"Some indians," I said, finally "must have told them."

"Well I'm glad to see you have a little sense anyway."

I asked him for precise directions to the pictographs but he shook his head. "No, if you really want to know, you'll find them yourself."

Earlier I had enquired about the story at the three largest universities in the province, and in three different departments. Most of those I spoke with had never heard the story of the Spanish episode; the ones who had some acquaintance with it, dismissed the matter out of hand and seemed to regard me as a troublesome crank. The professors in most cases, either gave me the brush-off or displayed an ironic and exaggerated politeness. One man insisted the

Spanish Mound story was nothing more than a tourist gimmick cooked up by the Osoyoos Chamber of Commerce. Another declared it to be a self-serving device of natives wishing to be regarded yet again as victims. The head of one history department insisted that the rock paintings weren't done until the late nineteenth century but failed to explain how he had come to this conclusion, never having seen them. I refrained from mentioning that every commentator on B.C. pictographs, white or native, from Franz Boas on, agrees that rock painting had ceased with the arrival of gold seekers in the middle of the nineteenth century.

It seems preposterous to insist that no European reached the southern interior of British Columbia until the 1800's. By the latter part of the sixteenth century, Cabeza de Vaca had already travelled overland from Florida to the Pacific northwest, and official expeditions from various nations had traversed much of the rest of the continent. These included an overland trek from Montreal to the Rockies.

Despite all this, and completely disregarding an entire body of literature concerning the pre–Columbian exploration of North America—much of it having to do with what would become B.C. —we are to assume that no hunter, fur trader, gold seeker, no soldier of fortune, naval deserter or escaped prisoner came overland from the south or east to the interior. We are also to accept that no one ventured more than fifty kilometres in from the Pacific coast; accept it even though the biggest prize in the history of exploration was the Strait of Anian, the mythical passage that supposedly split the North American continent in two. This route, which came to be known as the Northwest Passage, would have dramatically reduced the time and expense involved in trade between Europe and the Orient.

In 1570, the Flemish geographer Abraham Ortelius indicated on his great chart, the approximate location of what would become known as the Columbia River. No sooner was the map published than shipyards went into action, it being believed that the mouth of this river lead to the famous passage. But how did Ortelius know about the Columbia River?

In the next fifty years, the British Crown sanctioned no less than twenty expeditions to search for the river. The Russians, meanwhile, were sailing back and forth along the Pacific northwest coast, and the Spanish launched more than 150 coastal expeditions from Mexico in search of gold as well as the Strait of Anian. The most logical water route from the sea to the interior of B.C. is, of course, by way of the Columbia River.

In 1577, Queen Elizabeth I, dispatched Sir Francis Drake to sail to the coast of Oregon and from there to pursue an inland passage to Hudson Bay. Although Drake met disaster while returning south along the coast, there is still dispute over whether he got as far as the forty–eighth or the forty–second parallel. It is know for certain that at the northern extent of his journey, Drake put several men ashore who were never heard from again. The 48th parallel is the location of what came to be known as the Strait of Juan de Fuca, which was often thought to be the real entrance to the inland passage.

Hundreds of official expeditions set sail and many were never heard from again. Most of these, presumably, were lost at sea. The entrances to the Columbia River and to the Strait of Juan de Fuca are often referred to as graveyards for ships. It is not exactly a remote possibility that survivors of shipwrecks might have journeyed inland to avoid being enslaved by Coastal Indians or "pressed" by the next ship that came by, or maybe they simply wanted to see what was around the bend in the river.

The lost ships make for fascinating speculation. Beginning in 1560, numerous mariners claimed to have found the passage or to have run aground and, subsequently, to have crossed most or all of the continent. History regards these people as charlatans at worst, guilty of gross exaggeration at best; but there are a few whom hidebound historians cannot explain away and choose, therefore, to ignore.

After talking with Ernie Joesph in the Keremeos barroom, I couldn't help but think of one of the latter, a Greek mariner named Apostolos Valerianos, and of a scene enacted in another tavern almost four hundreds years earlier.

Back then the English consul at Aleppo was a merchant named Michael Lok. His hobby was financing expeditions to look for the Stait of Anian. Lok was behind Martin Frobisher's three trips to Baffin Island, and it was his dream to organize the party that would find the quick route to the Orient. Lok was, therefore, curious to meet a man rumoured to have travelled that very route not once but several times.

And it was a curious character indeed whom he finally encountered on the docks at Venice. The Greek mariner used various aliases but Valerianos was his real name. He swore that he had made the trips, the last just four years earlier, and if the English gentleman would stand him a drink, he would be glad to tell all about it. They repaired to the nearest tavern where Valerianos explained that he'd been shipping out of Mexico for the Spanish and had, in the 1580's, made three journeys along the northwest Pacific coast, finding what he was sure would eventually be recognized as the fabled route. Further, Valerianos claimed that in 1592, he convinced the Viceroy of Mexico to commission him on a new expedition. Lok wrote that the Greek mariner traced his route, "on a great Map, and a Sea Card of mine owne, which I laied before him."

Lok noted that at a point between 47 and 48 degrees of latitude, Valerianos followed the Strait to the north and east, and was led from one body of water to another, eventually crossing the entire country to the Atlantic Ocean. Immediately, he had begun the return journey to the Pacific, a trip that was not without incident, Valerianos being engaged at various times in conflict with the natives.

Lok believed him and set about raising funds for another expedition which the Greek would lead. But the money was not forthcoming, and Valerianos died, apparently of a broken heart. The man has gone down in history as a great liar. Yet, his geography in most cases was excellent. For instance, he indicated precisely the location of the Strait that he called Anian, since named for this unfortunate Greek mariner. But this Strait is not the Strait of Valerianos. In order to reach the city of Vancouver from the sea, one passes through a strait designated by one of the several aliases of a man famous primarily for being a liar, the Strait of Juan de Fuca.

There is a considerable body of circumstantial evidence indicating the probability of the Spanish episode near Keremeos. So called truths of history are often proclaimed on far less. Much of the material that got me interested all those years ago was collated by an amateur B.C. historian, later a provincial cabinet minister, Bill Barlee. Back then, I called him at his home in Westbank, and although he said he "he didn't believe the story implicitly," he reiterated his interest and welcomed more work being done. Barlee had observed that the physical appearance of the Similkameen band is different from neighboring tribes. They are generally taller and finer featured than others of the Salishan people. Even more noteworthy is the fact that the Similkameens are the only band in the Interior who can pronounce a pure 'r,' such a predominant letter in Spanish. What explains this ability and physical distinctness? Barlee was the first to wonder, in print, if it they might be attributable to the Similkameen's contacts with the Spanish.

Armour, made from heavy copper and perforated at the top of each plate, has been found in a native burial mound near Keremeos. The armour is almost identical in form to Spanish mail. Fur traders didn't wear armour and, so, if the Indians did not copy it from the Spanish, from whom did they get the idea? Also neither the Spanish nor anyone else wore armour in the nineteenth century. If the Similkameens borrowed from the Spanish, it had to have been prior to the early nineteenth century, the "official" time of first contact.

A number of ancient steel weapons have been found around

Keremeos. As well, the only piece of turquoise ever discovered in an Indian grave in B.C. was found near Okanagan Falls, which is where the invaders were supposed to have camped. The turquoise is still on display in the Penticton museum. The theory has been advanced that this particular turquoise pendant may have been carried by a Spanish soldier of the legendary expedition.

The Spaniards are said to have established substantial quarters in the northeastern part of what is now Kelowna. In 1863, the remains of a building, 11 by 23 metres whose cedar logs had been shaped with iron axes, was discovered northeast of Kelowna, near Mill Creek. A building of that size and design would likely have been used by a large number of men and horses. The natives certainly did not build those kinds of structures, and neither the Hudson's Bay nor the North West Company ever established substantial quarters in the area. The remains of the massive building were judged to be well over one hundred years old in 1863.

I drove west from Keremeos through fresh falling snow, stopping at a couple of houses where the occupants, natives, professed to be unaware of any pictographs. Closer to Hedley, I came upon two boys methodically shaping snowballs. One kid was white, the other native. Both knew about the pictographs and each pointed me in a different direction. The white kid wanted to argue with his friend. The Indian boy shrugged, looked at me and looked away. I got in the car and went his way. The white boy must not have liked it because he threw a snowball and hit the back window.

I stopped below the house that the kid had mentioned, a small place with a red fence bold against the snow. There I made enquiries of an elderly man and woman drinking coffee in their kitchen. They assured me I was close and added some details to my directions. The man had seen the paintings as a child. I asked him how old he thought they might be.

"Oh, heavens. They were known to be real old when I was a boy. There were old men around in those days whose grandfathers had seen them when they were children. They've got to be a few hundreds years old."

The couple's fat, goofy puppy followed me as I started my tramp through the fields, heading east from the house. It pranced at first, but slowed and stopped, baffled by the wall of snow. The puppy couldn't jump over the snow, so it tried walking through and was soon hopelessly floundered. Its master had to come to the rescue.

Once I located the old Great Northern railway grade, the going was fairly easy. A kilometre and a half along, past the remnants of a post–and–wire fence, I cut to the left across a field, and toward the cliffs. There was no trail but I found the place as if drawn by magnet.

I'd seen a bad photograph and a couple of drawings of the site, and assumed these pictographs would be smudged and indistinct forms that could, if one was so disposed, be taken as illustrations that substantiated the story of the Spanish travellers. Historians and archaeologists are forever constructing elaborate theories that become textbook truths on the basis of a fragment of bone or a few scratches on rock. Such things are then taken as gospel, learned by rote, and if one should ever see the fragment of bone or scratches on rock that are the basis for one of the That's Final dictums, one is, or at least I am, often put in mind of the old Peggy Lee song, "Is That All There Is?"

But back on that late–November afternoon, and each time I've been there since, I looked at the pictographs and was awed.

The face of the cliff leans forward at such an angle as to form a sort of grotto. In this protected place are several pictographs in two unrelated panels executed by different people which is obvious because of the colours, subject matter and level of skill. These sections are a metre and a half apart, the lower panel consisting of crude geometric symbols and representations of the sun. Higher on the cliff wall are the drawings that pertain to the Spanish episode. There can be no question as to what is depicted: two men hold the reins of their horses; to the right of them are four other men; there is a dog between the second and third man and above the heads of these figures are other dogs. The mouths of the dogs are open. All of this is as obvious to any observer as it was to James Teit, a colleague of the famous anthropologist Franz Boas. Teit published a description of the pictographs as part of the 45th Annual Report of the Bureau of American Ethnology, titled The Salashan Tribes of the Western Plateau.

But Teit does not indicate that the heads of the mounted figures are significantly different in shape from the heads of any other people represented on rocks in British Columbia. These men's heads are peaked and with pointed sides to indicate that hats are being worn, peculiarly shaped, to be sure, but certainly hats or, more accurately, helmets.

Every non–native who has commented on the pictographs is guilty of a glaring oversight. The four standing figures are joined by a line drawn through their necks. It doesn't require runaway imagination to suggest that these men are chained together and, hence, prisoners, and that the dogs, "with open mouths," in Teit's words, are guarding them, and barking.

According to the story that has been handed down, the Spanish invaders took several prisoners on their march to Lake Okanagan. Even superficial reading into the malignant history of the conquistadors shows that they had a mania for taking Indian prisoners whom they guarded with dogs.

The natives were kept chained together at the waist while working and chained by the neck during marches. The conquistadors were crazy about setting dogs on Indians, both for punishment and for sport. Diego de Salazar had a famous killer hound named Becerillo who, by order of Governor Ponce de Leon, received twice the pay his owner did, for every Indian killed or mutilated in battle. Becerillo's offspring, Leoncico, became the property of Vasco Nunez de Balboa, the man who 'discovered' the Pacific Ocean and who maintained a pack of vicious dogs used against Indians. While crossing the Isthmus of Panama, Balboa turned Leoncico and his mates loose upon a line of chained Indians. The dogs killed four hundred before the Spaniards grew bored with their entertainment. That dog pack was known as God's Avengers.

Shortly after my first visit, I wrote an article about some of this, an article that was vehemently criticized by white people, mostly academics, but was reprinted in various native publications. Years later, I was mixed-up in another contretemps over the story. It involved John Corner who, in the early Sixties, had produced the first book about rock paintings in the Interior. The book included his drawings and interpretations of the Keremeos Valley pictographs. In 1992, his book was reprinted to honours and applause. Speaking with me on the telephone, Corner politely dismissed the entire Spanish episode story with the familiar assertion that since the drawings show horses they had to have been done after 1750. Being polite in return, I did not point out that he was contradicting his claim in his very own book that none of the pictographs are less than 400 years old.

As for the line connecting the Indian figures, Corner told me it had to be "a pole or a boat." After I mentioned that none of the figures are touching it with their hands, he replied, "They didn't always represent things accurately."

Nevertheless, in this series of drawings the artist has taken great care to accurately represent a peak on each helmet, and teeth in the mouths of the dogs, and the way the reins flow into the hands of the riders. There is no variation to the arms and hands of the figures connected by the line, they are all done in the same way, hanging down.

Corner's comments lead me to the dissenting opinions of Glenn Douglas, a native researcher and librarian in Keremeos. Not only does he believe the story, he thinks he knows the precise location of the fabled Spanish Mound.

"If the story wasn't true," Douglas assured me, "it wouldn't have been handed down as truth from generation to generation."

So, over the years, I have returned to the spot, studied it, and, consequently, gathered more pieces of information. For instance, the iron neck collar the Spanish placed around their prisoners was called a cerebance.

On each visit, I had been particularly intrigued by the care with which the helmets were drawn. Not only was the brim, or lip, of the helmet distinct, the peak, as mentioned, was rendered just–so. I often thought of it. I learned that the helmet worn by conquistadors, and shaped exactly the same way, was a morion.

But my primary discovery occurred in Mexico, near Cuernavaca, on a cliff wall in country not unlike the dry land above the Similkameen River. I located an ancient pictograph that shows a soldier on horseback wearing a morion, and in front of him are five Indian prisoners guarded by dogs and chained at the waist.

These discoveries serve primarily for debate or discussion. My opinion was formed the first time I went to the spot, and it has not changed. I remember back then sitting on a boulder protected from falling snow by the vaulted face of the cliff, and observing the brilliant tableau before me, as others have surely done over the centuries. I knew then, and know now, that the story of the Spanish contact is true. This, as I am first to admit, is not exactly scientific methodology. But how is history determined and what is truth? Microfilm may melt, books disappear, files vanish and official documents blow away in the wind. Think of all the bugs, library larvae, nibbling centuries ago at texts that were already ancient. All that to me is so much folly.

I keep returning to the grotto, still a refuge these days even though the railway cut has been widened to allow the passage of hydro trucks, and less than a hundred yards from the pictographs is an unofficial trash dump. I have to laugh thinking of the timeless mystery side by side with the commonplace.

When there, I can feel the story in the stone, feel the truth being revealed to me. The truth is in the way the horseback rider holds the reins, the slack resignation of the prisoners, and in the tension and anger of the lines that form God's Avengers.

History, you know, is really a lie and changes its mind every day. Blood red lines drawn on protected cliff walls will last through millenia. In the end, the only historical truth is in the blood of the people. That's the secret of my own special place.

TALL TOM

I was in southern Alberta, driving into Okotoks, headed for Black Diamond and the road down to Chain Lakes park where I intended to pitch my tent for a day or two.

It was late afternoon on a clear early Autumn day. I'd been driving too many hours on deserted roads and my mind had begun to wander. I'd had enough of my own voice singing to the radio, I'd had enough of the radio which was full of the usual homogenized noise. I fantasized cowboys and Indians in the foothills, pictured a couple of roughnecks like John Wayne and Spencer Tracey striking oil and a boomtown growing up just over there. I flashed back to when dinosaurs rode this terrain.

I watched the headlight eat the yellow centre line, like I was holding down the button on a tape measure. I practiced the truck driver's arc. I glanced in the rearview mirror, the sideview mirror. What was over the rise, what had gone before. I was leaving myself and coming to meet myself. I had been driving too long. I hadn't eaten since morning. I could use a drink.

I found a place where I could get a meal and a beer. It was crowded, and most of the men looked like they worked on oil rigs or ranches. There were women in windbreakers and western garb. A few white collar types too, probably minor executives with the oil concerns. I had a table to myself, and ordered a beer and a veal cutlet. Not wishing to start a rumble, I had to have something to do with cows.

Four men at the table closest to me were talking enthusiastically about golf. They didn't look the type in their boots and flannel shirts. Their hands were dirty but it was honest dirt, don't you know. Hands that were used to gripping the reins of horses or being clamped around huge wrenches; hands that fixed machinery and were wiped on coveralls. I couldn't imagine any of those hands, grease in the finger creases, dirt under the nails, holding a nine iron or a putter. And years ago, they wouldn't have been. I tried to picture their granddaddies climbing down from an oil rig or a quarter horse, stepping up to the tee at some stubble field of a course where the hazard on the seventh fairway would likely have been a couple of Piegan with a pair of ponies and a baby on a travois.

I must have wolfed down half the meal and most of the beer before looking up from the table, and right into the eyes of a long and lean old man with a pink face and a pink bald head, white fringe of hair around his ears.

I went back to eating but after another couple of bites, hazarded another glance. He was also sitting by himself, and his knees were on a level with his stomach. The man had to be six-feet six. He was wearing a lightweight, pale blue and white pinstriped seersucker suit which was all wrong for the temperature outside. There were a couple of gaudy rings on his fingers and he needed a shave.

In my peripheral vision, I'd see him look at me, take a sip of his mixed drink and look back. Maybe he was an eccentric oldtimer who wore his summer suits the year round and had long ago bored all the locals with his stories and, seeing me, saw fresh ears. His face and his outfit appeared incongruous, putting me in mind of a hobo who'd won the lottery. May he was a hobo who'd won the lottery, some old bo I'd run into at the annual convention in Britt, Iowa.

If you look at anyone long enough, the person is liable to seem familiar. But it is also true that if one hasn't lead a life that offers scant opportunity for variety—as, for instance, a creative writing teacher—there are always rapscallions from the past who appear in one form or another at odd moments, often in bars, sometimes in washrooms, or even at yard sales. They're liable to telephone at three–thirty in the morning, although they always swear it's noon where they are. "Sir, I have a collect call for you from Frankie in Pohnape. Will you accept the charges?"—"Where's Pohnape?"—"The Federated States of Micronesia."—"Is Frankie male or female?"—"I can't tell, sir."—"Well [sighing] put it on."—"Hey, man. Remember me? It was Tok, Alaska, ten, eleven years ago. The roadhouse there? I bought you a couple of beers? Now here's the thing...."

The waitress appeared with another beer. As I extended the money, she said, "The old guy in the corner's paying."

I nodded to him, raised the glass. He stood up and walked across the lounge. When he got to the table, he seemed even taller than I'd thought.

"Thanks."

"Don't remember me, eh?"

His eyelids were long slits in the grizzled pink face, and I was put in mind of a lobster with white whiskers.

"No, not yet."

"I've changed a lot," the old man said, fingering his lapels and extending his hands so I could get a load of the rings."

"What were you like before?"

"Broke."

"Then maybe I do know you. Why don't you sit down."

It seemed like he had to fold himself in sections to do so.

"You were in a hell of a lot better shape than me," he said. "I was on the bum for sure."

"A bum where?"

"Still don't remember, eh? A bum on a beach."

"Oh, Fiji was it? That island, Taveuni?"

"Never been there." He shook his head like he was disappointed in me. "Try the beach at Playa Linda down Mexico way. Ring any bells?"

"Tom, for chrissakes!"

It was like a kaleidoscope spinning, the fragments finally snapping into place.

"All the time we spent together and you didn't make me straight off. I'm hurt, truly hurt."

"I'm sorry, Tall Tom but you got to understand, I've never seen you with long pants on before."

He was from these parts, I recalled now, and used to talk about his early escapades in Calgary, the Turner Valley, High River. His family had oil leases and ranch land all over the area.

The first time I ever saw him, Tom was walking down the beach carrying a fishing rod with a reel big enough to muscle in mythical swordfish. He was wearing khaki shorts and nothing else. He had preying mantis legs, spidery arms and a chest like a bone yard. We hit it off immediately.

"How's your wife?" he asked me that afternoon in Okotoks

"I wouldn't know."

He looked embarrassed; I changed the subject.

"I thought you vowed never to return to southern Alberta. Or anywhere in Alberta for that matter."

"Yes, there was only one thing that could have dragged me back. And believe me, I ain't staying."

Tall Tom may have been on the bum down in Mexico but he was no bum. He never put the arm on anybody, didn't cadge drinks and was always pleasant even when deep in the sauce. The only subject capable of fouling his mood was an older sister who was responsible, so he claimed, for robbing him of his share of the family's considerable wealth.

His father was one of those upper-middle class Englishmen

who arrived in the west for a spot of what they called big game hunting, took a look at those grasslands and those mountains, and recognized his future. The west was wide open then and the man took advantage. Besides ranching and oil, he bought up huge tracts of raw land. He bought vaudeville houses and theatres, and eventually developed a virtual monopoly on movie distribution. He was immensely successful and he was a thorough-going bastard. At least, he was to his son whom he decided to groom to eventually take over operations. According to Tom, his father's methods were heavy-handed at best and he was not opposed to raising those hands to his son. Perhaps if the man had been less domineering his son would have taken to the business but, as it was, Tom grew to hate his father and everything associated with him. But the old man's grip was so tight, Tom was thirty-two years old before he broke free.

Tom was the only son but he had a sister, Judith, who loved the family business as much as he had hated it. "You wouldn't call her feminine," Tom once said. "Always was sort of a, uh, Tomboy."

Or as the father was fond of saying—according to reports that reached Tom wherever his scuffling happened to be taking place—"That's girl's more of a man than my son'll ever be."

He would tell me all these things during long nights lounging on our porch on the hill surrounded by jungle or at a palapa bar on the beach called La Fortuna where Tom was stuck on a barmaid named Estrellita. He used to pledge his troth to her nearly every night. She was nice to Tom but it was obvious she thought of him as a funny, kindly man who was not as fortunate as other gringoes.

"No problema, Tom," Estrellita would say on the occasion of the near-nightly proposal. "I weel marry witch chew when, eh, you are a mee-yun-nair."

When we met up in Okotoks, it had been nearly forty years since Tom'd cut his ties and left Alberta. His savings staked him to two idle years in Hawaii which were followed by several busier ones. He worked at all manner of jobs there until deciding his money would go further in the Caribbean. It would too but that was in the Sixties. The father died around this time, leaving his fortune to his two children but Judith managed to have her brother declared—via some inbred small town legal maneuvers—incompetent to manage the money. So Tom spent his time knocking around the islands, crewing on boats, taking people out fishing, and washing dishes when times were toughest. He didn't make much money because he didn't have papers. But he always got by and managed to scrape together enough money to set an official foot in Canada every couple of years. Living was easy, whether it was in Barbados or on Barbuda, in Dominica or the Dominican Republic. By the time he qualified for his old age cheque, the islands had changed and Tom fled to Mexico. He'd been there for six years when I met him in Playa Linda.

"So whatever happened to your sister?" I asked him. "And how come you're back here dressed in this unusual manner?"

"Ah, dear, dear Judith," he sighed deeply, histrionically.

"Dear dear Judith? If I remember correctly you hated her. You never had a good word for the woman."

"I've mellowed lately. Come to recognize that indeed people change. Me and her, for instance. Judith saw the error of her ways at the end."

"At the end?"

"Yes. They buried her a couple of months ago. I just got here. Took that long for the lawyers to locate me. They sent a fax—you know that little store that sells helados and booze and has three phones and a fax machine across from the market?—yeah, so the fax says it is necessary for me to come up to Alberta to do the will business. I faxed back telling them to send me a ticket. I get this ticket in the mail one-way. I faxed them back that it is two-way or no-way. They had a return ticket waiting for me at the airport. That was three days ago. I expected the bastards to bill me for the ticket, especially since I'm now what you call a rich man, but they even charged me for the time and effort spent searching for me."

"Did you just say, Tall Tom, that you are now a rich man?"

"'Deed I am. Poor Judith was seventy-four and had been feeling poorly for some time. There was just me and her. She never married either. Hell, she didn't see the error of her ways and the old man's ways. There just wasn't nobody else to leave everything to. She didn't give to charities, wasn't the civic–minded sort. She put aside a few bucks for a statue to be made of herself in hopes the local powers–that–be would have it erected in a park or something. Otherwise, I mean, besides the statue and the lawyers' fees, it all goes to your old pal Tall Tom."

"Jesus. Oil lands, ranch lands, old theatres."

"Yeah, and six or seven houses, several apartment buildings plus three—or is it four?—mini-malls. Not only that but just between you and me, much of that which was ranchland when dear old dad snapped it up for next to nothing in the early days is now within the Calgary city limits."

"So you inherited...."

"Let's just call it a substantial sum."

"You could probably buy Okotoks."

"And High River too but who the hell would want to? Actually I don't know what I'm going to do with all that jack."

"Well, Tom, I could give you a few ideas."

"Ha! I bet you could. Hell, one thing, I'll tell them to let you do the statue of my sister if you want. But to be quite honest you ought to come back down to Playa Linda. I never forget a real friend."

"Thanks, Tom. Maybe I will. You don't have any plans to stick around here, eh?"

"No, way. I'll hire somebody to manage everything or sell it off. They'll take advantage of me but I don't give a flying–you–know–what. No matter how I spend the loot, it'll be spent down there. I'm gonna go fishing same as before, same as I was doing just a few days ago, but it'll be a nicer place where I lay my head at night. Evenings I'm gonna go down to La Fortuna same as always only I won't be nursing a couple of Negro Modelos all night. I sort of fancy trying those tall cool drinks in frosted glasses with paper umbrellas sticking up out of them. And you remember that good–looking waitress?"

"Sure Estrellita. She still there?"

"Yes, sir. And prettier'n ever."

"I remember how you used to tease her all the time. Propose to her nearly every night, and she'd say, 'No problema, senor Tum. I weel marry witchew when, eh, you become a mee–yun–nair.'"

"That's it, boy."

He took a swallow of his drink and smiled, parted those big floppy lips, "Well, little Estrellita, I can tell you, that girl is going to be some surprised when I get back to Playa Linda."

END OF THE ROAD

Now only the land is the same; that great Midwestern earth, rich and black along the beds of rivers like the Cedar that irrigate fields of corn and soya beans. There are many small towns like Britt scattered across the immense heartland of Iowa, Nebraska, Minnesota, Wisconsin and the Dakotas, and up into Manitoba and Saskatchewan. Once they were all connected by freight lines. The oldtimers say it used to be "real hobo country." In those days steam ruled the rails and the Iron Horse called at each of these towns to take grain and livestock to the great railheads. There was plenty of work for a knight of the road and always a sidedoor Pullman to catch out of town. But alas, this era too has just about chugged to a halt, and it owes its passing to more than the coming of King Diesel.

It was a Great Northern boxcar I was jockeying with a "bo" named Floyd Wallace (alias the Greeley Kid), some 30 years my elder, the first time I hit Britt in 1965. I knew the rails, the blinds, the crumbies and the camps, the monikers and the tall tales. I was acquainted with the vast land and a feeling of absolute freedom I've never been able to recapture for more than a flickering instant.

Thirteen years ago we skipped out of that dirty, dark, maroon boxcar and into the tall weeds by the silos in Britt and made our way to the municipal park to rustle up some stew and see if there was anyone about we knew. They were all there then, bragging to the locals and feeling more than a little legendary. There were real bos in those days—Bigtown Gorman, Sweetwater Gibson, Liberty Earl (from Liberty, Kansas, not to be confused with Liberty Ike from Liberty, Pennsylvania), Jack the Painter, Baseball George (who shadowed the St. Louis Cardinals around the country) and the Hardrock Kid who, if memory serves, was crowned king that year. Even Seldom Seen Slim was in attendance. Real old bos, boomer workers out of the past. An age was dying, but the old boys were still scanning the horizon.

This time, however, I'm driving into town in a brand new rental car with a plastic dashboard, and all the motels are filled. The Hardrock Kid, John Mislen, is buried on the edge of Britt, and Bigtown Gorman is about to breath his last in a ward at Northern Iowa Medical Centre in nearby Mason City. A year ago up in the Yukon an old bo told me Floyd Wallace had up and died, disappeared actually, and indicated that his end might have come as a result of watching the disastrous transformation of certain events of his roustabout life onto the silver screen in Emperor of the North, starring Lee Marvin as a guy a lot like Floyd.

A hobo is not a mission stiff (wino or bum), nor is he lazy. Very few lazy people would survive the rigors of riding a cross-country freight or the other hardships of freedom. A hobo is a boomer, a transient worker. Many of the first hobos were railway workers who kept on travelling once the last spike was hammered. They would do any job at hand, but they wouldn't make a habit of it. During the lean years, if a man came around to your back door and asked for a lump (handout) he was a bum. If he asked if there was any coal to be shoveled, furniture to be moved, mowing or haying to be done in exchange for a meal, he was a hobo.

The Iron Horse required constant replenishing of its coal and water supply, as well as numerous pit stops to shake the fire grates down. This meant a stop every 100 miles, which enabled the knights of the road—also known as members of Tourist Local 63—to hop aboard. Whenever you saw a water tower you'd know there was a hobo camp or jungle in the vicinity, not only because the trains stopped there but also because the tanks carried plenty of water for cooking up the mulligan stew, brewing coffee, bathing and playing Chinaboy (doing the laundry). No matter where a jungle was located a fellow would be sure to find it in neat order, with pots and pans, eating utensils, mirrors, maybe a couple of chairs or car seats, a cache of food and reading material. Notes with messages and greetings and general information on jobs and flops and travel plans would be stuck to the tower beams or pinned to trees.

Every 100 miles a hobo had a home. Diesel power and sealed container cars have retired most of the knights of the road (as Floyd Wallace used to say, "Not even God could hop a high-ball at 70 miles per hour"), and old age has caught up with many of the remainder. And there aren't many new boys coming down the line to replenish the breed. The reason is, as any bo will tell you, the homogeneity of modern life. It's hard to be a hobo in a franchise world. Not to mention the sad fact, according to Fred Charles, alias the Cheyenne Kid, that "people aren't as friendly as they used to be."

In the late 1890s the old hobos took to meeting every year in Chicago for what they called a convention but was actually just an excuse to cut up jackpots and feast and socialize. When the city fathers of Britt learned about this annual do they invited the hobos to hold the next convention in their tiny town. The then king of the hobos, Cotton Onion, agreed, and the fourth convention of Tourist Local 63 was held in Britt on August 22, 1900. The convention was planned as a one-shot affair to get Britt a piece of publicity. After 1900 the locale switched from one town to another, anywhere that could be reached by freight train—Fort Dodge, Kansas City and Altoona, Pennsylvania. In 1933 Britt decided to celebrate the anniversary of the historic event and it has remained the site of the convention ever since. The king that year and for a few thereafter was Hairbreadth Harry, who was so inspired by wearing his coffee-can crown that he wrote a book, a sort of spiritual outpouring called Inner Tubes Come Clean. His throne was usurped in 1936 by Tom McDougall, alias Scoopshovel Scotty, who cooked up a particularly delicious stew that made the other bos feel it was better to have a good cook than a literary genius for a king.

There was a different breed of bos back then, full-time knights they were. Their heydays were the '30s and '40s, after which North America settled into its relentless pursuit of material goods and tract houses and became paranoid about men who shunned this new way of life. They're gone now, men like King Ben Benson, Roger Payne (the hobo philosopher), Cannonball Eddie Baker (prune picker and wandering slumgullion mixer), Highway Johnny Weaver, Texas Decker, Jeff Davis and Old King Cole.

But this year there is only one man who can be called a legitimate hobo and that is Frisco Jack, an ex-merchant seaman who is probably 60 but looks 40 and has been everywhere. Dressed in denim, with a red bandanna around his neck, Jack is a throwback to another era. He rode the rails and goosed the ghost (hitchhiked) down from Alaska and graciously avoided the hype and ballyhoo of the convention. When they are voting for king he is nowhere to be found.

The only other real bo around is the Cheyenne Kid, who, because of his age is restricted to about three months a year on the road. He admits he rode the hound (the bus) to Britt from his home in northern Minnesota. "See, if I would've come by freight I would've had to travel around and about and to hell and gone to get here and it would've taken me days. Can't ride a straight line no more. No, sir. But I've done my share of knocking about. I started out in 1927. And I've always been proud to let people know that I'm a hobo. I'll be with some people and one's a shoemaker, the other's a steelworker, and they'll ask me what I do and I'll tell them I'm a hobo. They can't figure it out because I don't look like a bum or a derelict and I'm not a wino."

Cheyenne is sitting on a bench under a tree near the siding. He looks toward the other claimants to the crown and the people thrusting microphones in their faces or sighting them through viewfinders. "Used to be the festivities were held in the middle of the week, but the town switched it to the weekend so more folks could attend and spend their money."

And it used to be that the hobos would pick a king from among their number. Now the candidates appear on a stage in the park, and each gives a speech and the king is picked according to the applause he gets from crowd, so that it is merely a popularity contest. Among the 12 aspirants this year there are two hippies, two winos, one who admits he has never ridden a freight, and Hobo Bill Mainer, a railway historian.

The 1977 king, Sparky Smith, gave up riding the rails a few years ago due to ill health and isn't standing for re-election. There's a kid from Richmond called Virginia Slim who has hitchhiked around the country and uses his speech to plug his poems of the road. That leaves Lord Open Road, a burly, good-natured character who is now almost exclusively a hitchhiker; Pennsylvania Kid, who wears an outrageous hat with feathers and is fighting tooth and nail against age and senility; Hobo Adam, whose expenses to the convention have been paid by the San Francisco Chronicle; Cheyenne Kid; and the perennial favorite and eventual winner, Steamtrain Maury Graham.

Now, it's been a long time since Steamtrain hopped a freight, and, as any oldtimer will inform you behind his hand Steamtrain was never more than a dilettante. But he looks the part: he might have stepped from an 18th-century lithograph of Father Christmas. He is short and roly-poly, dressed in a black blazer adorned with 100 buttons; a red bandanna is tied around his neck and he sports a gnarled walking stick. He makes a speech about all the other places he's made speeches in over the years (he's done the college circuit and Sun City, and the crowd loves him. The journalists interview him until he pleads exhaustion and retires into a trailer to rest and get a drink and, for all I know, call his broker.

Hobo Adam is phoning in an interview to the Jocko Thomas

radio show in San Francisco. Cheyenne is availing himself of the barbecued pig the town has provided. The press isn't paying any attention to him because he doesn't fit their image of a hobo: he doesn't have a beard and he carries, of all things, a cassette recorder. Frisco Jack is still in hiding.

When Hobo Adam, also known as Mr. Nobody or Adam Ydobon (which is nobody spelled backward), returned from his interview I asked him if I didn't recognize him from San Francisco in the late 60's. He grinned, stroked his beard, and said "Yes, and you know I'm 79 now."

Then Mr. Nobody tells some stories of the road and Frisco Jack reminisces about London and Rio. Lord Open Road, who always speaks in rhyme, comes upon the scene toting his duffel and saying, "I've been down the line and I'm feeling fine. Yes, sir. Been dealing with the local citizens but of course they're not really denizens of this sort of life. Mainly, I'm disposed to suppose, because they want to avoid the strife. Um, hum."

He pauses to lick his lips and frown. "Had breakfast this morning. Waitress wanted $3. Had a couple of eggs blinded."

He looks at me. "Know what that means?"

"Sure, Over easy."

"Two on a raft, float' em?"

"Poached on toast."

Lord Open Road is still on the road, hopping a freight when he is able but more often thumbing or just plain tramping. He maintains an address, a mail box at a hotel in Kansas City to which he returns every month.

As I stood talking to Open Road, the memories flashed by like the carloads of teenagers in my peripheral vision. Floyd and I had ridden a sidedoor Pullman into town and made for the jungle which was looked after by Pop. Floyd and Pop and the others reminisced and everybody chipped in to make a supper. Later that evening while the oldtimers were jawing, I set out on my own to discover famous

Vine Street, where Pop had been born. I was literally, as the song has it "standing on the corner, Twelfth Street and Vine," when I got arrested. When I hadn't shown up the next day Floyd figured what had happened and took up a collection to pay my fine. The next day we parted at the bridge. He went up to Port Arthur, and I headed out to the coast. I never saw him again. The next I heard was that Floyd had just up and disappeared. He had been living in a room in Pismo Beach, California, and one day he went down the road for the paper and a cigar and he never came back. He might have drowned or got hit by a car but there was no report of it. I prefer to think he really did disappear, just as I hope all the other remnants of the legend, when their times come, will just disappear down the road instead of dying in miserly rooms or old folks' homes. When that way of life vanishes something bigger will die, because the hobo knows the one absolute freedom, a feeling you can't get unless you sit there in a boxcar watching the prairies and mountains roll by in endless variety and infinite wonder.

"When the tourists leave the bulls'll make us move on," says Lord Open Road.

"We'll have served our purpose."

Cheyenne Kid watches the television crew and declares, "I'm not coming back here anymore."

It was time to get out of Britt.

The next day I stopped at a railway crossing in a small town in eastern Iowa to let a freight train rumble by. There was an endless string of boxcars, boxcars, boxcars, all of them sealed. But near the end, back by the crumbie, a flat car was loaded with brand new automobiles. I thought of Floyd Wallace up there in hobo heaven where there aren't any bulls and none of the boxcars are sealed. I could see him leaning back in the front seat of one of those brand new automobiles on a flat car, preferably a Cadillac, smoking a big cigar and watching the world roll by down below. Just high-balling through heaven day by day by day.

STREETS

To be born in the street means to wander all your life, to be free. It means accident and incident, drama, movement. It means above all dream.
Henry Miller

DANCER

It was a weekday in late October, warm, the sun shining. For nearly a month, everyone had been sure that the weather was going to change any day now, any hour, but it hadn't. This particular day it was just so warm and so beautiful that there was a bittersweet feel to it, as if this had to be the end of it. The streets were crowded because everyone knew.

There was a vacant table outside Pastel's on Robson Street. I had been loitering all over town and figured I might as well stop one more time.

Two people were at the register waiting for the kids to fill their orders. They rubbed against each other and whispered sweet nothings back and forth. They were both women, girls, really. The smaller one was in orange sweats and had a blonde femme haircut. Her companion wore a padded-shoulder jacket and black shirt, dyed black hair arranged in a big pompadour and wings. Give her sunglasses and shades and she'd pass for Roy Orbison.

Standing there waiting my turn, I wondered about them. Sure, of course, I know that some people are born that way just as others are born other ways, but sometimes life has a hand in it. And these two were so young.

The one in the orange sweatsuit shot me a nasty look. I must have been staring. I didn't take it personally though because her hostility was too general, encompassing all of my kind.

Her partner looked where she was looking, filled with territorial propriety and ready to duke it out. We held a stare. She was about 5'8" and solid. Then, just as it was getting a mite awkward, her expression changed. The hostility was replaced by curiosity, although not friendly curiosity.

"I know who you are," she said.

"You do?"

"We've met before and I've seen pictures of you."

"Yes?"

"Yeah, you used to fuck my mother."

She told me who her mother was.

"Do you remember my mother?"

"Don't say it like that. It's been a long time since we've seen each other. Twelve, thirteen years."

"Twelve."

She turned to her companion, pulling back the flap of her sport jacket. There was a thick silver chain connecting a belt loop to a black leather wallet in her back pocket. "Do me a favour, eh? Get a coffee somewhere else and meet me back here in half an hour."

The girl shot me a pouty smirk and walked out. We sat down at the counter.

"I remember that day at the airport," she said. "It was raining and I was soaked."

"Yeah, you were in your pretty new dress and didn't have a coat on. It's strange but I remember your shoes. They were like a grown-up woman's shoes."

"I was quite the little lady. I didn't know whether you were going with us or not. Then my mother turned away and grabbed my hand. She had tears in her eyes."

I hadn't seen the tears.

"'The last I saw of her she/was reaching for the ceiling/and a guy with a badge was/running the gadget/all over her body.' Ah well, that's from this poem I wrote about your mother and me."

There was a hint of a smile then, just a little wrinkle in the corner on one side of her mouth. "'She looked up at me/with those big, wide eyes...'

"Yeah," she said. "I used to have the fucking thing memorized. 'and I saw tears/seeping through mascara...'"

"So she must have seen the poem too."

"She bought the book in Saskatoon, out by the university. I came across the poems because my Mom kept the book hidden in my room so my father wouldn't see it. It would have given him another excuse to beat us. Not that he needed any excuses."

"How is she, your mother?"

I had to get around to it eventually.

She gave me the flat-eyed stare, and I thought, "Oh no."

"My mother's dead."

I met her in an elevator at the St. Regis Hotel in Vancouver. She had on a short, satin robe like fighters wear and it was covering bare skin. Or, at least, so I imagined, judging from the long, bare legs beneath it. She was about 5'11" in her heels, thin, lithe. It might not have been love at first sight but it was something close, and lust only partly. She got off two floors before I did. We had merely nodded but she glanced back as she left the elevator.

She was an "exotic dancer" downstairs, that much was obvious. The next night, I looked into the pub and saw her on stage divesting herself of her garments and her legs went on forever. There was a certain unfeigned innocence to her face which was absurdly incongruous to the positions she assumed. The men watching maintained a weird decorum. There was not the usual commotion, faces didn't wear the typical expressions. She finished to energetic applause.

I didn't know what I was going to say to her when she came out into the lobby to get in the elevator, or if I was going to say anything at all. I doubted she'd even remember having set eyes on me. But she smiled as if she was genuinely glad I was there. We hemmed and hawed and tiptoed around each other on the red and black carpet, and I noticed her shiver in the satin robe. "Let me go up and change," she said, "and then you can buy me a coffee, if you want to."

There was no hemming and hawing at the Chinese place around the corner. I felt I could tell her anything. She seemed to feel just as easy with me.

She had escaped a husband back in Saskatchewan; he would get drunk and beat her, sometimes he even cuffed their daughter. This behavior started not long after they were married and it only got worse.

One night her husband came home with a load on, convinced she had men in while he was at work. He knocked her down the stairs. "I had a black eye and a cracked rib. It could have been much worse; it was only seven steps."

The day after that incident, she took the daughter and moved back to her mother's place, a farm 100 kilometres from town. But the husband came after them.

She fled to the coast then, taking her daughter but leaving the little girl with a cousin in Hope.

"I feel so guilty about it."

"About being separated from your daughter?"

"That, of course but I mean about leaving my husband."

"But you might have gotten seriously hurt if you stayed any longer."

We drank coffee until the man started snapping off the lights. Enough coffee to keep us from sleeping, if we'd thought of that.

Dawn had made its appearance by the time we returned to the St. Regis, to her room. There were not many days during the next three months when we were not together and most of these occurred the first two weekends that we knew each other. She had to make the bus ride to Hope. She didn't want her daughter to come to town and see where she lived. Finally, she'd saved enough money to get her own place, an apartment at 5th and MacDonald. "Dancing has been good to me," she said as we cleaned the apartment prior to the arrival of the little girl.

When mother and daughter were reunited, I kept out of the picture for a few days. I was a little afraid that everything would change between us, but it didn't. We became closer than before.

My own relationship of three years had ended a few months earlier. I travelled out west thinking I would never find anyone who came close, and now, unexpectedly, I had.

And one evening, just as unexpectedly, when I called at the apartment, I saw it in her face. "What's the matter?"

"Nothing's the matter."

We went to a movie nearby, at the Hollywood, and walked home afterwards. "All right," I said. "Let me have it."

"It's my husband."

The man had been seeing a psychiatrist; he'd stopped drinking and was attending A.A. Her mother wrote that he was a changed man. He'd gone to see his mother-in-law, broke down in tears and begged her forgiveness. The woman wrote that he deserved another chance.

"If my mother says it, I have to go back."

"Do you love him?"

"It's nothing like with you and me." She hesitated, bit her lower lip. "It never has been."

We had our final scene at the airport less than a week later. There, with the little girl in her new dress looking up at us, I had my say. For a moment I was sure she was going to buy it, but then she came out with something so unlike her, "I've already checked my bag."

And she turned, grabbed the little girl's hand and went

clicking away. The last I saw of her, she had stepped through the box and a guy in a uniform was outlining her body with the gadget in his hand.

It would all have been a perfect memory except for that flippant remark.

"She said that on purpose," the little girl was telling me now, twelve years later and dressed like a man. "She told me she did. She wanted you to think less of her so that it would be in your mind if you ever got the notion to come looking for her."

I almost had gone looking a few times. But we'd made a deal. Good–bye, no regrets. No three in the morning phone calls. Nothing. It had to be that way. She had to have her mind clear to make a go of her marriage.

"If you had come for her, she'd probably still be alive. She had this stupid idea she owed it to society to make her marriage work. But it's a stupid men's society and she was just another victim of it."

The daughter took out the truck-driver wallet again and showed me a newspaper clipping that had been laminated. "A couple of months after we were back it started again. I was fourteen when he killed her."

"So it lasted another six years."

"Yeah. Six years of hell. Sometimes she'd see these things you wrote in that magazine that came with the papers. She wanted to find you but you were always in Africa or someplace and she was afraid if she started making inquiries, he'd find out and make it worse for her. He got ten years. He's in with that scum bag, the premier's son who killed his wife, too. He'll be out in a year, my father. Time off for—catch this—good behavior."

I read the clipping and stared at the picture. Who were they talking about? A person I'd known? It gave their address in Saskatoon. It was all so petty and stupid and tragic. Succinct and laminated.

The girlfriend was back. The daughter stood up and I handed her the clipping. "Men make me sick. I hate them all."

68

The girlfriend giggled.

"But for whatever it's worth," she said. "My mother, what she thought about you, she really..."

She couldn't finish it. She hurried out and the other one followed after. I watched them cross Robson Street, their arms pulling each other close.

I went out then into the late October sun that had no business shining, and thought, for whatever it's worth, I had felt the same way about her.

PAGES FROM THE

SIDEWALKS OF LIFE

"Well, Lorsie, I just came home from work, it is 9:00 O'clock at night, I went to work at 6:00 O'clock this morning and if you remember I got your letter at noon and I spent noon hour here at my desk answering it and did not get any dinner. Jackie was in the kitchen, it looked like he had been making hamburgers, I ask him if he had any left and he said no, so Lorsie when you are making a nice supper for Wilfred just think of your husband comming home to a cold kitchen. Lorsie I am crying so hard I can hardly see for tears."

That comes near the end of Glen's letter. He's in New Brunswick and Lorsie is supposed to be in Toronto, having run off with Wilfred. Somebody named Thibodeau told a guy called Allan that Wilfred hadn't really wanted to take her to Toronto, that he really—and this is Glen writing to Lorsie—"just fed you a line to get you into bed." Not only that, but this operator Wilfred, gossip has it, tried to split to TO without her, so Glen tells Lorsie she better be careful of him because "he may not ever be as good as me and

Toronto can be a lonely place alone."

Then, the very next line, Glen brings out the only thing in his arsenal, telling Lorsie: "I am sorry but I cannot let you have any of the boys." He claims it's because he doesn't think Toronto's a good place for them, and he reminds her that she "subjected the kids to a lot more suffering than necessary."

Glen adds that she might as well save the money it would cost to "come down" to New Brunswick unless she wants "to come back to me." Otherwise, she's not going to see the boys. They "are the only thing that keeps me from killing myself."

All this is on four small sheets of notepaper, written with ballpoint pen. There were seven other pages, but I only have VIII to XI, and the writing isn't cramped; thus, an entire human drama is condensed into just a few sentences. I found them 10 years ago near the railroad tracks out back of the Princeton Hotel on Powell Street in Vancouver. I have hundreds of other pages that I've found on streets all over this country, and other countries too. It was just the other day, reading Glen's letter, going through my collection of these letters and notes, that I realized I was behaving just as the Count had done all those years ago.

I take these letters out every so often to wonder about the people involved, how the situation came about, and what they are doing now. Take Glen. At first, he seems quite pitiful, what with the woe-is-me routine and him playing on whatever feelings of guilt remain in Lorsie. He sounds like a bad country song. But what if you picture his wife, cooking, cleaning, shuffling the kids around all day, and here he comes in the door, late for dinner, liquor on his breath and feeling frisky?

You might think she's well rid of him, but, on the other hand, there is the matter of those kids, "the boys." Lorsie just up and left them. How many and how old? Say there are only two of them. I'd bet that Jackie, cooking hamburgers, is one of them. If he is and he's cooking hamburgers at night, and Glen doesn't complain about the cost of baby-sitters or getting his mother over there to help out, you have to figure the kid must be 15, and even if he is the oldest of "the boys," it means that Glen and Lorsie aren't exactly kids. If Lorsie split after all those years, she must have been either desperate or seriously in love, or both.

Something else that makes me feel for Glen is that he signs off, only to add something else under his name. He does this twice in four pages, as if as long as he's writing, he's somehow connected to this woman who's breaking his heart.

Now, because I didn't find this letter in Toronto but in Vancouver, another series of questions presents itself. Did Lorsie and Wilfred only pretend to be going to Toronto, so Glen wouldn't know their whereabouts? If so, it was not a spontaneous act, because they had arranged to have their mail forwarded. Or, perhaps, no sooner did Lorsie get to Toronto than she realized her big mistake but was too ashamed to go home. Maybe Wilfred really only wanted to get her into bed after all. Perhaps she used this would-be Lothario as her way out of a bad marriage. There are variations on each possibility, plenty to ponder.

It is almost 40 years since I travelled with the Count, thirty-nine-and-a-half years since he sat down on that bench in Lockport, New York, and quietly read that letter—violet ink on rag paper—and proceeded to comment on the people involved in the story it contained. I remember it was from a girl who had gone away to college and was writing to her hometown friend. The Count said she seemed to be putting on airs, and instead of impressing the Lockport girl, perhaps she had alienated her, alienated her so much that she tossed the letter away, thereby effectively ending the friendship.

The Count went on about all this, brow knitted, studying the letter, tapping the tip of his chin with the outside of his right index finger, as he was in the habit of doing, and considering all the possibilities. And I see it all now as if a movie: the distinguished tramp with the Russian accent and his 13-year-old runaway juvenile-delinquent companion discussing a stranger's thrown-away letter and surrounded by the citizens of Lockport, walking, driving, going about their quotidian errands.

And the camera pulls back and up and away.

I met him in Niagara Falls at the American end of the bridge. It was four weeks since I had turned 13 and six weeks since I ran away from home. I was trying to figure out how to get into Canada without papers when this character who looked like a rugged version of Ronald Colman came striding toward the U.S. of A., tapping a cane before him, wearing a short leather jacket and an ascot in August; the toe of one of his army boots was wrapped with electrician's tape.

I laughed. He gave the macadam a peremptory tap with his cane, fixed me with an imperious gaze—but there was a twinkle in his eyes—and asked, in a peculiar, to me, accent, if he might inquire as to the object of my mirth. I asked him if he was with a troupe of wandering players. He said that there was no troupe; he was the whole show. It seemed natural to fall in with this guy whose last name I remember as being something like Navrotolov.

In downtown Niagara Falls, he made an abrupt right turn into an alley and headed directly to a huge trash bin, returning after a couple of minutes with two pieces of paisley silk about a foot square. One he handed to me: "A *foulard* for your shirt pocket."

I asked him if this was the first step in becoming a real fool. He stared at me a moment before nodding. "Quite good."

This was the first indication I had of this strange character's dedication to cast-off items, not to mention his unusual past. I got a glimpse of the latter when, after muttering about not having an outside pocket, he unzipped his jacket: there, pinned to the lining, were at least a dozen combat and commemorative medals. Being a wiseass, I asked him if he'd gotten them at a pawnshop. "Indeed not," he said, and he proceeded to tell me about the various battles and countries each one represented. Later, when we met a Russian buddy of his, I discovered it was all the truth. He'd served in the military of three or four countries as well as one hitch with the French Foreign Legion.

We walked. The Count wouldn't thumb a ride for fear of being trapped and bored. He picked things up off the streets and the roads, told stories, and I found him curious indeed.

"Why," he said to me that first afternoon, "when I was your age, I had a dogsbody."

And I answered, "Oh, well, you look all right now."

"I beg your pardon?" he replied, perplexed.

Half the time, I didn't know what in hell he was talking about. Like when he called me a kobold or a larrikin. But I soon realized he didn't know what I was talking about half the time either. For instance, once, when a yellow convertible passed us somewhere southeast of Onondoga, I exclaimed: "Hey, a Corvette with two girls in it!"

"What! Surely not a corvette. They've been obsolete for decades."

"No, man. They just started making them five years ago This one was brand-new."

"Oh, you mean it must have been loaded on the back of some sort of truck, being hauled to a museum. But what about the girls. Were they ancient WAVES?"

Much of the conversation was like that, but a lot of it had to do with his experiences. Most of the Count's family had been wiped out in the 1917 Revolution, and he was part of the vast dispersion of White Russians throughout the world. When I met him, the Count was returning from Toronto, where he went every summer to visit a childhood friend. The other man had been a serf on the Navrotolov estate. The Count's father provided the boy with books and tutors. Later, the Count's friend, having resisted the wishes of the Bolsheviks, was imprisoned but managed to escape, only to wind up in a refugee camp in England. Eventually, the guy managed to make it to the mines of the Canadian North. In 1958, too old to get a decent job, he lived in a rooming house in Toronto. The Count laughed bitterly, ironically. "Yes, the nobleman and the serf. The revolution succeeded in making us equal."

He found a rubber toy soldier that first night. A little green guy with a helmet and a rifle with a bayonet. The Count looked at it closely, put it in his pants pocket, but took it out every so often. "Does his wife miss him?" he wondered. "Or is she keeping time with another?"

The next morning in a coffee shop, he left it atop the chrome-plated napkin dispenser at our table.

Once he nabbed a piece of white paper from the roadside weeds and hiked along looking at it. I didn't pay much attention, but having seen it was just an advertisement of some sort, I wondered what could be holding his attention.

"Tell me," he said finally. "Is $11.99 a good price for a tune-up?"

"Yeah, Count, it's pretty good. You thinking of getting one?"

"No, I am in splendid physical condition."

One day, he began talking about books and was horrified to learn that I was not a reader. Turning solemn and serious, the Count pleaded with me to begin reading as soon as possible. I promised that I would. He mentioned writers that he had known in St. Petersburg, Paris, Vienna. Alas, I can't remember any names.

We came to a shopping centre, and while the Count made the rounds of the bins, I waited on top of a low wall at the parking lot's perimeter. As a car pulled away, I noticed a paperback book between the white lines. Not only was the back cover missing, so were most of the pages. It was a novel about sailing ships. When the Count returned, I handed it to him, saying, "You probably won't want it on account of it ends on page 73 in the middle of a sentence."

"Doesn't matter in the least. The book is like life itself."

We slept in fields, on the beach at a lake resort, in a maintenance building that someone had forgotten to lock at a high school, but that night I curled up in a banquette booth at the diner across the highway from the shopping centre. The Count retired to the split-level in back with the widow who owned the diner, but that's another story.

It was early the next afternoon that he found the letter from the girl who'd gone off to college. The Count explored the story the letter revealed from all possible angles, much like, I didn't realize then, a novelist putting characters through their paces. He took the story and its implications very much to heart. What if, he wondered, the local girl wasn't angry at all, didn't think her friend had become stuck-up at her fancy college? Maybe she envied the girl her escape from a stultifying small-town existence, seeing herself stuck in Lockport, a supermarket-checkout girl the most she could hope to be.

"Yeah, Count, but in that case, why'd she throw the letter away?"

"Perhaps she lost it. Imagine her tonight, everything quiet and exactly the same as it always is outside her bedroom window, but somewhere far away at college, all is new and exciting and life has promise. Ah! With what anticipation she prepares to read the letter from her friend! But, alas, it is nowhere to be found. Her distress!"

"Yo, Count, don't get so worked up; you don't even know these people."

The Count admonished me right quick. Told me that it wasn't necessary to have met them. That he had empathy with them. That in imagining their lives, he felt connected to them and that was important, him being a guy just passing through.

He told me that it wasn't always convenient for him to have a book in his pocket, but it mattered not in the least. "For, you see, these," he said, shaking the sheets of rag paper between his face and mine, "these are the true literature, these letters I find lying about. Yes, my great regret is that I have not been able to maintain a collection over the years. Being peripatetic, you see. Ah, but that would have been wonderful. Perhaps I might have printed them in one volume some day. I have found them everywhere. Particular favorites I carry about on my person for weeks, months, years, in some cases, tucked away in my billfold. Joyful, commonplace, unnerving, pretentious, tragic, excruciatingly boring, and comic. Again, like life itself, and that is the point and why I pick them up. I would call my book Pages From the Sidewalks of Life. What do you think of that?"

"Yeah, Count, that's great."

I didn't appreciate what he was saying then. Or, at least, I didn't seem to, but the message, the meaning of it, must have penetrated my subconscious, because there I was, 13 years later, walking down Pendrell Street in the West End of Vancouver when I glommed on to a piece of paper on the sidewalk and stooped to pick it up. It was an invitation to a dinner given by the lieutenant-governor of the province. I continued along toward Denman Street, wondering what the woman had done to warrant the invitation. There was no "Mr. and Mrs." on the invitation, so, if she wasn't single, her husband didn't come into the picture. Had the dinner been arranged to honour only women? If not, I was surprised such invitations didn't include guests. I was in the middle of mulling these matters over when I remembered the Count. I hadn't thought of him when picking up the piece of paper, but damned if I wasn't acting just like the guy.

And from that day to this, I have, like him, kept an eye open for these stray missives. I don't pick up laundry lists or shopping lists or advertisements, just correspondence between actual human beings. Unlike the Count, I have hundreds of these within reach, three thick folders on the desk now. But, like the Count, I have had to discard hundreds more (along with books, music, and artwork). Occasionally, it has been necessary to leave a place quickly; other times, stuff was left in storage and never retrieved. Hundreds of pavement pages. Here's the opening of a letter found in Vancouver in 1995: "Stephe—Things have been crazy here. Barrie turned to stone —9-5 in a junk art gallery—new clothes—doesn't associate with the likes of me. Really miss her but I write better songs now."

Maybe he does write better songs. "Nine to five in a junk art gallery" certainly has potential.

I found this in Toronto in 1979, even though the date pencilled at the top is Tuesday September 7, 1965: "I am 9 years old and I live at 140 Zaph Ave. I have 4 brothers and 2 sisters. My father works at CPR and at Canadian Gear. I'm four foot six. My telephone number is AT 282-6456. I weigh 72 pounds. We have dog and a cat. We had 20 rabbits and five chickens but we let the rabbits go and ate the chickens. My friends are Jimmy, Gordy, Norman, Moran, Doug, Sidney, James, Van, Joey, Tom, Dave and I like all sports."

He'd be in his 40's now. I wonder what his life is like. That was a big family, but the economy would have been good for another 15 years. How tall did he get to be? Four foot six is pretty big for a nine-year-old. (Or what if he didn't grow?)Did they let the rabbits go on Zaph Avenue? Are Gordy, Norman and the rest still his friends?

Why did I find that letter or homework assignment 14 years after it was written? Could he have kept it all those years only to have it go astray during a move? Or maybe he died young and it was his mother's cherished keepsake.

In the late '80s in the laneway between Granville and Richards streets, I saw a large manila envelope on the ground. It had been run over by a truck. Perhaps it fell from the heaped-up trash in the dumpster that was nearby and the wind had blown it down the alley. In the envelope were a dozen or so letters from B.C. and Washington state, all relating the sexual experiences and fantasies of men who enjoy being dominated and humiliated. Evidently, the letter writers paid the recipient—who advertised in a sex-trade publication—to send, as it were, a response. A letter writer might be permitted to graduate to a session of in-person humiliation and domination. The correspondents are male, but one claims to be writing with the blessing of a girlfriend who wishes to be included in some hot bondage action.

The fantasies, with one exception, are heterosexual. Most of
the letter writers seem to be middle-class, "respectable" types. There is
a lawyer, a jogger and rock climber, a biology student. One man
writes, in part: "I am a submissive white male, age 58, and 220 lbs. I
am a former catholic priest. I am also divorced...For the last 20 years I
have served Dominant Mistresses in Ontario, in the States, and
occasionally in Germany. I began doing so when I was still in the
priesthood. I had fantasized of being bound and humiliated since age
8 or 10. As a priest in the confessional I found out I was not alone in
this field...I have felt the cane, the whip, the strap, the paddle as well
as the old-fashioned hairbrush. My ass was not the only target. My
back, my tits (rather big for a man), my inner thighs have felt the heat
of the spankings...My nipples have experienced the squeeze of clothes
pins. My cock and balls were encased in a spiked harness...I have been
humiliated by being spat upon my face. I have been baptised with
Golden Showers. I have suffered the pain of an enema."

The letter is signed, "Submissively yours."

Generally, when sexual or romantic longing is expressed in
the pages I've found, it is done in more subtle ways. Here's one picked
up in 1983 in Vancouver, although dated December 8, 1971 (it is
curious that so many of the letters are from years before):
"Kelly—This is your Gilpin old lady. I'm still in Gilpin—but am
leaving in a matter of a couple hours. The snow is coming down like a
mother fucker...Later—now I'm sitting in the pub with all my stuff
waiting for either a ride all the way to Seattle or a bus. Everybody out
Gilpin way is stoned or getting there."

This letter was of particular interest to me because I
happened to arrive at Gilpin about seven months after the letter
writer, Cris, got a ride out of there. I used to sit in that pub too, in
Grand Forks, waiting for a lift anywhere, as long as it made Gilpin a
memory.

Ten kilometres from Grand Forks, Gilpin, in the early '70s,
was an abandoned Doukhobor community taken over by hippie

squatters. I didn't know this back in Toronto when my best friend wrote me saying it was all very beautiful, the river right at the door of a cabin on which no rent need be paid. I'd have a great time. What I found when I got there was a sort of totalitarian hippie Dogpatch. Everyone went around naked and scowling, looking for infractions. I imagined them at night listening at the cabin door as if hoping to hear me or my buddy—we were the different ones—say something nasty about John Lennon.

"Why did you get me out here?" I asked Marcel, who was broke.

"I was stuck and bored out of my mind," he said.

"Great, now we're both stuck and bored out of our minds."

Cris went on to tell Kelly: "You really made me feel content and good about myself while you were here. I just wish I could have lived up to it. Me & Henry talked about it and we figured that I'm actually shy about sex. Sounds pretty weird, eh? I've always found it hard to totally give myself to someone. Mainly because I'm not sure of myself. And I didn't want Peter to stay that nite. But I found my head all screwed up about you staying with Linda. But now I know that was stupid."

My friend had been holed up in Gilpin for several months before I got there. I've often wondered if he knew Cris. She seems too nice to have hung around that hirsute Hitler youth camp unless she, too, was stuck. She closes her letter to Kelly: "I hope you don't get all fucked up in the city. Find somebody good to take care of you. Home cooked meals, etc. Don't be too surprised if you see me at your door some day. Anyway—I'll write even if you don't answer. Love, Cris."

Dear Donny, I live with my mother as she is divorced. Sometimes I dream I am living with my father, we live in your building and we are very rich.

You are from a country called Glip. When you meet someone, you must always speak to them with your noses almost touching, otherwise people will be greatly offended. You only accept things from people if they place the object on the floor before you & stand back. Nicole.

This is neat. Mr. Stadenko just pulled us over...Steve had a big fat gram joint in his left pocket. We were stopped because we saw Colin in his parents' Explorer. We were comparing weed when the cop was turning left to go up towards the highway and he saw us and backed up to turn around as soon as we saw him we walked towards Steve's car and Colin took off. That's when the cop pulled up behind us, turned on his lights and well the rest is self explained. Cool.

I also pick up parts of letters, bits and pieces. Someone suggested I go through the trash containers at post offices, but that seems like cheating. One scrap has four words: "Happy happy, joy joy." I also have a page retrieved from a fire, upon which is typed a "Code of Chivalry." Torn pages and parts of pages can be arranged to make William Burroughs-style cutouts. This one is composed from two letters, one found in Kelowna, the other in Vancouver: "My home is located on the touchy area of Naramata, a contemplative self-image allowing me glances tough it is for most /of the animals and birds age and experience. A short time ago the fact that an extremely affluent neighbouring country gradually and at our security guard at the gate helps Verge of an overwatered /subject matter. I was observed by, as well as comfortable for me endless stream of golf in and out one's own and close to my patio. Specific information in precious water racing a pace from on high."

In my compendium of stray sheets, of back-alley scribblings, of pavement epistles are more lovers' lamentations, as well as postcards to the home guard ("We made it! Spent last week just lounging around the campground...On our way to Banff today. Planted our crop." Planted our crop?), accounts of the what-I-did-on-my-summer-vacation variety ("There was a spa and everyday interesting things to do in the Bavarian countryside"), numerous religious imprecations and pronunciamentos ("Satan has many deceptions to offer deluded souls. Kingdom Hall [*Watch Tower*] is one of the most seductive!!" as well as "I am Satan"), notes to the Ministry of Social Services ("Welfare. Re: John Buck. Go to Apt.7.") and letters from the logging camp ("I am working for D. Dumaresq in the lake above Rivers Inlet. I have been on the D8 up until last week now I am driving a new Kenworth. They also have a new steel Madill and the American grapple").

There are also poems:

> *i cannot return*
> *upon knees begging*
> > *in rabbit clothes*
> > > *you tore out my heart and splattered enamel on it*

But there are fewer personal pages of any kind to be found these days. This is not, as has been suggested to me, because there is less littering now. No, I don't believe that these letters and stray pages were tossed away on purpose. It is simply that most people don't write letters any more. Used to be, back in the early '70s, I'd come up with at least one personal missive on any walk around Vancouver or Toronto. Months will go by now before I find anything. People don't take their e-mail outside and drop it on the street. When are they ever on the street? And who would want to read it anyway in its impersonal uniformity? My notes and letters are on every conceivable type of paper in all sorts of printing and handwriting and typing. They're joyful, commonplace, unnerving, pretentious, tragic, excruciatingly boring and comic, these pages from the sidewalks of life. Just like life itself. Just like the count was always saying.

"We lost Vina (Stanley's wife) in June. & we miss them both. Our friends get fewer each year as we get older....Keep well & have a Blessed Christmas time and good New Year. Jean & Gordon."

"Hi! I am sorry for not writing sooner. I seem to be always

busy with my cabin. I am 20 years old & live in Surrey. Come see me on the boat & I will tell you the rest of your questions. Tanya. PS: Thanks for EVERYTHING!"

"A lot of the camps have shut down already, it's going to be a long winter. I would grab that mill job if I were you...Keith wrote once this year. I have been expecting another but it hasn't arrived. Let me know how you make out...Take care. Love, Dad."

As for the Count and I, we continued on our way, reaching the home of his friend Koscheff in another town in upstate New York. Koscheff was a sallow, blubbery figure with spittle lips and dandruff. He ran a mail-order business in ancient maps and books on cartography. Koscheff was not of the Count's class, a fact about which he was defensive. He told me that my pal Navrotolov, because of his scrounging habits, was called Count Garbage behind his back. This creep Koscheff rarely left his home, it being the height of the Cold War paranoia and him a known Russian. But he had agreed to drive the Count to the wealthy town of Cos Cob, Connecticut, where another Russian aristocrat had offered him a "position." Nominally, he was to be groundskeeper of her run-down property. This was, no doubt, a polite way of offering the Count a home, if he wanted one.

Our ways parted near the turnoff at Schenectady. As I stepped out of the car, the Count handed me a piece of heavy paper folded in four. It was a large photograph of himself, from his salad days, in full-dress French Foreign Legion uniform, chest festooned with medals. There was the imperious gaze and the twinkle that indicated he was only kidding. He had signed it with a reminder to remember to take up reading.

Later, I framed that photograph, divided into four parts by creases, and for years it hung on the wall of whatever Toronto flat or room in which I happened to be living. I trust the person who stole the photograph of the Count from my place at 56 Howland Avenue in 1973 appreciated it. In hopes that she eventually threw it away, I keep my eyes peeled.

Perhaps someday it will turn up, there on the sidewalk.

THE HIT MAN

There was a quarter of a million dollar contract out on him, and he had taken to hanging out at my house in Vancouver. The people who wanted him eliminated weren't shopping around for a killer. The offer was in-house, as it were.

These people did not stick cotton in their cheeks and wear white ties with their black shirts. I remember one day when he was telling me about his employers, the crime bosses of Toronto, a couple of brothers. Racco would call him on the phone, say "Go make sure this guy doesn't show up at the trial...scare the shit out of so and so, break his legs if you have to."

I said to my new pal, "What does he wear, Racco? A guy who gives those kind of orders?"

"What's he wear? He wears running shoes."

"The head of the Mob wears running shoes?"

"Yeah, that's right. Casual clothes."

I had heard of this man whom that organization, known to non-Italians as the Mafia, wanted dead, before I ever met him. He was a biker recruited by organized crime to take care of special assignments like arson, intimidation, extortion, robbery and murder. He plied his trade for a few years, but began to be bothered by his conscience and the intuition that his own days were numbered.

He told me this in the most unlikely of places, the basement weightlifting room at the main branch of the YMCA.

He realized he had to get out of a group from which one does not resign. "When I got involved I was at a point in my life where I didn't care what happened to me. I knew I'd be killed sooner or later, but it didn't matter."

He went over. He was given a new identity in exchange for testifying against the crime lords. He was in the midst of this when I met him.

His lawyers thought his story would make a good book. Somebody gave him a copy of a novel I wrote called *Streethearts*, and he said, "Get me this guy."

I was summoned to Toronto and brought by cops to a hotel room.

One might have taken him for a well-off businessman who plays rugby on the weekends. He had a perm, a neat moustache, and favoured those shirts with a little animal over the breast pocket. The only thing that didn't fit were the eyes. His eyes were small and hard and they held you.

We sparred around and decided we could get along. The deal was that he would know where I was, but I could not know how to reach him.

A couple of weeks later, I got a phone call in Vancouver. He came out to the house and we ate spaghetti.

He'd be around for a few days, then disappear. He had a girlfriend in Vancouver. He kept a ten-speed bike at her place and would pedal it to the YMCA. He had huge arms and shoulders, pectoral muscles like a breastplate and slender legs. My wife said she knew women who would kill to have legs like that.

He smiled a lot, but it was a sad smile. Only once did he laugh like he meant it. We were getting dressed after working out, and he was telling me a story about breaking some guy's arms and setting fire to his warehouse. He finished the story out on the street. Then he climbed on to his bike.

"You ought to get one of these ten-speeds," he said. "Why don't you? They're neat."

"No, man. I got my image to think of."

He laughed. He was laughing as he pedalled off up Burrard Street in the sunshine, like a guy without a care in the world.

A couple of nights later he wanted to go out for a drink. He left it up to me to pick the kind of place where we wouldn't run into the wrong kind of people. "This is the first time in two years I've been out at night with another guy who wasn't a cop."

There was a longing in his voice. In back of those knowing eyes, beyond all that muscle, he was desperate. He was one hard case, but with someone like that, the other things stand out all that much more.

I remembered from the papers that he had blown up a restaurant and a cook had been killed. I asked him about it.

"One of the guys, his wife had been in there for lunch. She didn't like the way the maitre d' spoke to her, and she complained to her husband. He called me up. 'Go blow the fucking place up.' I'm sorry about the cook. He wasn't supposed to be there that morning. Chinese guy."

He regretted the things he had done, but he didn't try to justify any of them, ask for forgiveness, or remind me how bad he felt about everything. For my part, I didn't moralize or shrink from him. Neither did I try to signify that I was real tough, too. For these reasons we got along.

He told me about placing a bomb next to the rear tire of a Montreal mob leader's car. "It was in the parking lot under his building. Every morning he went down there, got in his car and drove to town. I set the bomb, and what happens? The first morning in ten years he doesn't go down there. He's sick and sends his valet on an errand. Guy lived though."

One evening, I ran into him on Granville. He was coming out of a movie theatre. I had already seen the picture, Nick Nolte as a news photographer in Nicaragua. "How'd you like it?" I asked.

"Terrible," he said. "All that shooting and they never reloaded."

Things were going well with our book. There was a wealth of the kind of material that makes for what the reviewers call a "terrifying but thrilling read."

There wasn't anybody in the bunch he talked about who, in any way, resembled Cagney, or Raft, Pacino or De Niro. These were guys who, if you looked at their wives the wrong way, would murder your children and leave you alive to think about it.

He told me the only one he respected as a man was Paul Volpe, the one-time crime boss. Volpe hadn't changed with the times, so it had been decided he should be dumped. My partner went to Volpe and told him about it, even though the man knew he had turned.

The publishing company, alas, blew our cover. One day I answered the doorbell and saw a guy who looked like he had been cast for the role of Mob mechanic. There was a car at the curb bearing the name of a courier service. The Mob gets into those kinds of businesses. He took a large envelope out of his pouch and said my partner's name. "Is he here?"

He was there all right, sitting in the kitchen drinking coffee. The man with the envelope fixed me with a flat, dead stare. If I was doing a movie, this is how I'd set up the hit scene. Guy takes a gun out of the courier bag and pops me. My partner bolts out the back door, right into the thunk-thunk-thunk from the machine pistol of the guy in the alley in the silk suit.

What could I do? I said, "I'll sign for it."

He handed it to me, walked down the steps and turned to give me a funny look.

My pal took the envelope and stared at it, shaking his head. It was to him, care of me. "They just don't realize, the publishers, they can't connect what I'm talking about with real life."

Thus ended our professional collaboration. He went right out to his girlfriend's car and drove back East. Somewhere.

Eventually he found another publisher and another writer and the book came out. I hope it does well and makes him some money. I hope that he is still alive.

I did see him again. He came back to Vancouver, and we hung out some more lifting weights. One day he called and said he was going back for good, but he needed a couple of suitcases and cases for his guns.

We hit all the thrift stores on Hastings Street. "How about a nice shirt?" I asked him. "Or this powder-blue polyester leisure suit here. They'd never recognize you in this."

There was still the matter of the gun cases. We tried a few sporting goods stores without success. I told him of another place. "But I don't think you want to go out there."

It was on Commercial Drive, but he was all for it. He knew who lived there, having come out several years earlier to grab a payroll meant for a fishing fleet. "They wanted somebody from outside."

After we got the cases, he wanted to walk down Commercial. I fell in step. He looked at me with surprise. "You're coming with me?"

I shrugged. He liked that. He mumbled something about not having any friends. I didn't catch it all, but I didn't ask him to say it again.

He caught a plane the next day. I never saw him again, but he telephoned one more time, the day after he got back. "The Toronto airport was filled with cops. A couple of hours before I arrived, they found Paul Volpe's body stuffed in the trunk of his car. They thought I had something to do with it, but I told them I had an alibi. We were at the gun store."

JIM CHRISTY

DIANA BAD... SELF-PORTRAIT IN PRATER PARK

I n spite of myself, the Vienna I imagined was the usual melange of Schubert and the Empire; vineyards above the Danube; coffee in the company of old fellows who'd known Hugo von Hofmannsthal personally; threadbare octagenarians reminiscing about the claque at the Opera; a rendezvous at the Hotel Sacher with that widowed countess who'd given the slip to a dashing young Hussar with his medals and moustaches—he was handsome and could offer her vast estates but she could never respect him, knowing he'd permit her to walk all over him—there were midnight carriage rides through the Prater, and when the wind blew, stars glittered through a lacey canopy of tender almond leaves...

That song that had been big a couple of years earlier, "Those Were the Days," seemed redolent, to me, anyway, of Vienna. I didn't know then that it was originally a gypsy song. Nevertheless, it made me think of the mid–Thirties just as the heel of the jackpot was descending, and all these years later, two lovers meet by chance in some dive with beaded curtains; shabby but genteel, they'd survived with little but their dignity. Alas...

I had a girl too, but she left, taking most of the money with

89

her. To be honest, I let her take most of the money, and it was not because she fell back on that "I'm just a girl" routine (which she did) nor tried a play on my pride: "I know you. Drop you on any street in any city in the world and you'll make out just fine" (which she did). Neither of them worked. I just let her have most of the money, that's all.

It had begun to unravel a month and a half earlier, in Rome—she'd never been away from home at Christmas—and it came apart completely one morning in the WOK Cafeteria there in Vienna where we'd gone to escape the freezing streets. The first thing to be seen was an octagenarian cashier with a mouth like a painted anus. She had a plunging neckline and the loose flesh of her wrinkled chest was folded into a black lace and steel-enforced brassiere. But it was her open-toed elfin pointy boots that seemed the most obscene.

We had to make our way through a section of the cafeteria reserved for war veterans, stepping over wooden legs in the aisle, being watched by men who, instead of hands, had metal hooks clamped on mugs of coffee, to a table in the back. No sooner were we seated than a pair of diesel dykes noticed Lorraine and stopped nuzzling each other to give her sultry stares and flick their tongues. Lorraine bent her head to a plate of Schwenfurt cheese, sauerkraut and pumpernickel bread and didn't want to look up. But I watched everything, watched as a man removed his hat and two overcoats, smoothed down his thinning, dyed black hair and fingered the indentations in his skull. From one suitjacket pocket, he took a half-smoked cigar and an ivory holder. From the other pocket he brought a plastic box the size of a paperback book. He removed the lid and turned the box over. A dozen or so prophylactics spilled out and he lined them up like soldiers on the table top.

I nudged Lorraine. She looked at the guy. He noticed, narrowed his eyes, arched one brow and leered at her. His teeth were yellow. So much for breakfast.

"I'm going back to the hotel."

Lorraine got into bed under three blankets and declared she was staying put. Everything out there was just too horrible and she didn't know why she'd been crazy enough to leave Canada anyway.

I went back out to wander, went into coffee shops, into St. Stephens and the public reading room across the square. Then, like an idiot, I walked halfway across the city to see a bleak, miserable little park where Hitler'd given a speech one time. When I couldn't avoid it any longer, I returned to the hotel. Lorraine had gone through three quarts of beer and half of Erich Maria Remarque's novel about Lisbon which I'd found in a junk shop in Belgrade. She announced she was leaving by train the next morning. She drank more beer and became sentimental, and I assumed she would change her mind in the morning.

She didn't. I walked with her to the train station. Across from the Westbahnhof, about a dozen North American hippies spilled out of the Zoch Hotel and sprawled on its steps. One of them looked up from his guidebook and droned a question, "Wanna buy some dope, man?"

"No," I answered.

"How bout you, lady?"

"Go fuck yourself," Lorraine advised.

There was no dramatic farewell. Not a kiss goodbye either.

The train pulled away and I walked outside again, thought about what I was going to do, and decided to head on over to Freud's house in Bergasse Street. Why the hell not?

The house was cozy. The great man's umbrella was in its stand in the narrow hall. The leather couch looked comfortable. I liked the oriental rugs and all the carvings. There were no velvet ropes. You kind of expected him to walk in at any moment, just come from the cigar merchant's.

I was all right until I left Freud's house. Outside it was the crepuscular hour, exactly the right, or wrong, time to begin thinking about a woman who's run out on you in Vienna. In an attempt to dispel the approaching darkness, I splurged on a decent meal only to feel like Jackie Gleason's lonely guy amid the happy diners.

Later, I turned into a little place on a sidestreet just off the Opera Ring. It was all brown wood with a long bar, lamps with beaded shades hung above the tables, and maroon satin curtains could be drawn across booths for privacy. A large, middle-aged man in a black leather trenchcoat that looked like it could drape one of the lesser alpine peaks, was sitting by himself at the bar, and after a few minutes I tried a little German on him.

"Jeez, pal. That was awful."

He had a New York accent.

"Well, okay, but you look Austrian as all get out."

"My ancestors. I still speak the language which is why I'm in town myself instead of sending one of my men. Big soccer match today. I don't know much about it but then neither do most of our readers."

He was the sports editor of an international English-language newspaper based in Paris.

"Yeah, I thought it sounded like a wonderful idea," Paul Waggoner said. "Living in Paris and working on the paper."

"You're not obsessed with all that Hemingway-Fitzgerald nonsense, are you?"

"Hell, no. I see myself more along the lines of Joe Liebling in the City of Light."

He patted his ample belly.

"And it is kind of wonderful except for the sports they got. Bike racing, auto racing. Tennis. I farm out all that which doesn't leave me much to do. The occasional boxing match. Then I began looking around for oddities. You know, six foot ten inch black kids from Camden, who can't make the NBA, playing for Milano in the European pro league. That kind of thing.

"People over here don't know anything about baseball, alas. That's my sport. Always has been. Used to cover the Yankees and

Mets back home when I was on the papers in Jersey. Jesus, if I was home now, I'd be packing my bags to go down to Lauderdale. Pitchers and catchers are all ready on their way."

But Waggoner was not the obsessive homesick American eager to latch on to anyone who spoke his language without a British accent. He asked me about what I was doing in Vienna and seemed interested in my story about Lorraine but that wasn't anything I wanted to dwell on so I got him back, eventually, to the grand old game.

He was old enough to have grown up in the Depression, dreaming of becoming a big leaguer. "There were great players in those days. Greenberg and Gehringer, the Gashouse Gang. Hack Wilson was still playing. Jimmy Foxx."

The place filled up as we talked but I hardly noticed except for one woman who was probably a few years older than Waggoner. She was elegant in a grey silk and gabardine suit, no blouse or sweater under the jacket. The woman turned her head away from the bartender and when she saw me, her polite smile vanished. I thought she was annoyed so I averted my eyes while Waggoner talked, but I felt her staring and looked again. She didn't smile, didn't frown, and there was certainly no invitation. Then the bartender was there and she was in control again, nodding to him, arranging her napkin, giving her drink a stir. Waggoner was talking about the coming season's pennant race.

I hardly had enough interest left in modern baseball to keep from seeming rude. When he got on to the subject of old timers versus the new guys, I was able to join in. "Listen," I said, "if Ty Cobb was around now, he'd hit six hundred..."

"Excuse me, please, gentlemen..."

I don't know how long we'd been going on like that before the woman appeared in back of us. "Please, but I cannot help being curious as to what it is you are talking about with so much enthusiasm."

She was holding her glass at her waist; her nails finished with clear polish.

"Why baseball, madame. Our national past time. Or, at least, it's my national past time. He's Canadian. But they play it there too."

I noticed the thin silver bracelet at her neck. Her skin was tanned and smooth.

"So, you are Canadian?"

I was confused, the way she looked at me, not sure of what was in her expression. She almost seemed afraid. Surprised, certainly. Or maybe I was imagining too much.

Waggoner asked her, in German, if she would care to join us. She answered him in German, then looked from the bar stools to one of the booths, gestured toward it with her empty hand.

"This would be more comfortable for conversation, yes?"

Waggoner and I got up, and we moved over to the booth, him motioning for her to sit first. She smiled and said she preferred to be on the outside. After Waggoner and I had taken opposite sides of the table, the woman sat down next to him.

"Again, gentlemen, I ask you to pardon my intrusion. It must appear unconventional to say the least. But I am simply curious. It is so very rare in this country to see two men speak with enthusiasm to each other about anything that is not politics, and most often that particular enthusiasm turns to hostility."

Waggoner nodded, told her how well-loved baseball was "back home." Told her that it united people of all ages and racial backgrounds, and did not inspire riots as did European football matches. He explained that this had to do with the pace of the game and its history with which most Americans, though sadly, fewer and fewer, were intimately familiar.

"Why, ma'am, baseball stars are our country's mythological characters. We have no Zeus, no Odysseus." It occurred to me that he was testing the spring training essay, every sports columnist's annual excuse to get poetic. "Instead, we've got The Mighty Babe and The

Splendid Splinter, Dizzy, Daffy, and Pistol Pete."

She made a good show of appearing interested in all this, nodding in the appropriate places, smiling at the colourful nicknames. I pictured her during intermission at the concert, or the reception at an embassy, under the chandelier, light sparkling off her jewelry, entertaining the local upper crust with anecdotes about quaint Americans called Wee Willie and Three-Finger Brown.

After an hour had passed, Waggoner glanced at his watch and sighed. "Well folks, it's been lovely but I have a story to get out on the wire by midnight, so I'm afraid I'll have to bid you a fond goodnight."

"You are sure you cannot stay a little longer?" she asked with polite disappointment.

He said he was late already, suggested I look him up in Paris, and walked off with a little wave.

We both watched him go, as if we mustn't dare speak until the door had closed behind him. But even then she said nothing, just stared at her folded hands. Finally, I said I should probably be going as well.

"Oh, no." She reached over, touched my wrist, kept her hand there for a moment and asked me if I liked champagne.

"Yes? You do? Why then..."

The waiter brought the bottle and she pulled the curtain closed, saying that champagne nightcaps were a local custom.

Once more, she endeavored to assure me that it was not her habit to initiate conversations with strange men in taverns, or anywhere else, and had only stopped in because she was early for the theatre. Finding our conversation so "enchanting" and having seen the play already, she decided to stick around.

Then it was my turn to excuse myself.

"Here I am in your country and you have to speak my language."

"Oh, I learned English because it is necessary in my work."

She operated as a liaison between artists and industry, and

travelled frequently to North America. "I sell the works of my artists, my clients, to large business. These concerns have fortunes—at least, the money seems like a fortune to the artists—but the people in charge have little, if any, taste. I try to present myself as a consultant rather than an agent although that is what I am, really."

She reached for the pack of cigarettes Waggoner had left behind, made an awkward job of shaking out the last one, and fumbled for the pack of matches that was tucked behind the cellophane. It took her four matches to get a light.

"I only smoke when I'm nervous," she said, tilting back her head and exhaling smoke.

"You know I'm a failed painter. My experience, however, allows me to talk with artists and buyers. I enjoy my job immensely. I think perhaps you have done some painting. Is this so?"

"Some, yes. I'm more inclined to sculpture, collage. But I don't do much art work."

"Can you draw?"

"Not in the 'draw like an angel' sense."

"Ah, but what does that have to do with anything?" She made a dismissive gesture with her cigarette hand. "Me, for instance. I can draw perfectly well but I have always lacked the, what is it, the basis, the originality...In German, it is much better: ursprunglichkeit. That certain something that is essential to a true artist. If you are not a visual artist I feel sure you must do creative work of some kind. Maybe you yourself do not know this yet. Yes? Someday you will make the discovery. I can see it in you. In fact, you remind me of someone I knew who was an artist, a very great painter. He could have drawn the left–hand angel of the Baptism in the Uffizi."

She stopped talking to summon a waiter for more cigarettes and said nothing until he returned and lighted one for her.

Her eyes were the exact grey of her suit. Her hair, mostly black but with more than a little grey, was brushed back from her face. When she smiled, a small comma appeared at each corner of her mouth.

"Listen to me, please. Before the war, I knew a boy here in Vienna who was a painter. His name was Rolfe. He gave lessons at his studio and that is how I met him. He was so alive and in love with his art. In love with life. We became great friends. May I ask how old you are?"

"Twenty-six."

"Yes, I knew it. That was his age."

"You didn't know him very long? Just that year he was twenty-six?"

"Yes."

"Why just that year?"

"Why? It was 1938. Hitler drove down the Mariahilfer Strasse. Kristallnacht. Rolfe was Jewish. Rolfe was taken away. I heard no more of him until after the war and what I heard was of his death in a camp."

"Were you in love with him?"

"Oh, yes. In love. Very much. He was the love of my life."

She looked at her hands. Looked at the champagne glass.

"I am talking too much. I must go home."

I began to tell her how much I had enjoyed meeting her but she cut me off saying it would be bad form not to at least offer to escort her home.

"May I see you home?"

"Yes, indeed. Thank you."

As we pulled up in front of her building, she admitted that she could stand one more drink after all, it being so cold.

"Perhaps you would like one also?"

The small lobby had a marble floor and mirrors in scalloped frames. The elevator man's jacket was the same maroon as the curtains at the booths in the tavern.

There was a small fireplace in her livingroom and windows that reached to the ceiling. Glass doors gave on to a small balcony and, looking out, I could see the bare limbs of trees silhouetted on the snow of a little square. Tables held carvings and art deco lamps that put me in mind of Freud's living room. There were oriental carpets of different sizes on the parquet floor and paintings covered the walls above the wainscotting. I recognized a small Paul Klee and asked after a larger painting. "That is done by a man name Hundertwasser who has only recently begun to get anywhere near the notice that he deserves."

She asked me to light a fire, then excused herself and left the room.

When she returned with a tray of drinks I was on my knees examining the pattern in one of the carpets.

"That is over one hundred years old."

"But the colours look so fresh."

She set the tray on a white leather Ottoman.

"Once a year, at the time of the biggest snow fall, I carry my rugs down to the little park just over there. I turn the rugs over and let the snow cover them. This I saw the peasants do in the mountains of Afghanistan. After a few hours, I brush away the snow and take up my rugs. They are now clean and onto the snow has been transferred the pattern of the rug."

We sat on the floor, leaning back against the bottom of the sofa, sipped cognac, and looked at the fire. After a few minutes of talk about rugs and paintings, she said, "Please, listen to me. It was not your conversation with the other man that made me speak to you. It was you yourself. This is quite extraordinary, more than you know. You see, my friend that I was talking about, you remind me so much of him. So very much. It is, for me, as if time has been turned back. I am sure you understand what it is that I wish you to do."

Later, when she got up and left the bedroom, I heard her moving about in the apartment. I was drowsy, luxuriously so. I drifted off and woke as she got back into bed, put her arms around me.

"We never did that, Rolfe and I."

It was growing light outside when she asked me to please leave.

"I know you are probably confused. It would just be impossible to sit across the table from you and try to make conversation while we have coffee. And I could not bear the emotion of seeing you ever again."

She watched as I stood by the bed putting on my clothes.

"I am trying to memorize you," she said, and reached to touch my hip.

"I know you must be confused. There is something for you on the fireplace. Open it only when you get back to your hotel. Then, I believe you will understand everything."

When I finished dressing, I said goodbye but she buried her head in the pillow and said nothing.

I took the package from the mantle above the fireplace and left the apartment. The lift appeared with a different guy in maroon and no expression.

It was bitter cold. At the corner, I saw that the name of her street was Diana Bad. I hopped on a tram car filled with people going to work. All the way across town I stood with one hand holding the strap, the other feeling canvas and a light wooden frame through the wrapping paper. I wondered if she had made me a present of the Paul Klee; it was too small to be the painting by the other man, Hundertwasser.

Back in my hotel room at last, I opened the package. The painting was by her friend Rolfe. It showed a man and woman at Prater Park in 1938. They were standing in front of the big globe of the world and above their heads in the background was the top of the giant ferris wheel. Although the woman was twenty–three years younger, there was no mistaking her. I recognized the man too. Looking at him, I was looking at myself.

LOST IN THE UNIVERSAL SEA

He was bent over a sink in the washroom of a bistro on Bernard Avenue in Kelowna in the Okanagan Valley of British Columbia. Long, grey hair hung below the collar of a black leather coat that was as scuffed as the sorriest pair of shoes at the bottom of a bin at the Sally Ann.

He looked up then and our eyes met. His still glittered above cheekbones that looked like they'd been stuck on as an afterthought. The face was gaunt and lined, the neck wrinkled as befitted the old man he had become. When he turned away from the mirror, I saw that the coat was kept closed by a belt from a fat person's pair of pants. At his feet was a cheap rucksack.

He shook his head as I started to talk, taking a pencil and tiny notebook from his side coat pocket, and handing it to me. "Deaf now," he said, "Can't read lips yet."

"It's been a long time," I wrote.

He nodded, "Yeah, man. A long time."

He had made his first couple of million by the early 60s, a time when a couple of million still meant something. When I first encountered him more than twenty years ago in Toronto, there were still a few bucks left and he was all shining eyes and bristling energy. The first thing he ever said to me, he sang, "It's fun, it's fun, to be a part of the Universal One!"

I was in bed at the time. His face was a foot from mine. His breath smelled of cigarette smoke with a hint of fish. It was a hell of a way to be woken up, even if you knew the person. I had never seen him before. "Um, huh? What the?" I said.

"Yes, it's me. It's me, just another fish in the great big sea."

I raised my head a little as he began a shuffling dance around the room, chattering, his fingers sketching on the air.

"Yes, indeed, we are all part of the Universal One but not all of us know it. Well, perhaps, in an intellectual sense some of us can grasp the idea of a community of Man and Woman but few of us really know. Conversely, some of the most enlightened ones have no knowledge they are on the Main Road. Heh! heh, heh!'

He was turned out in chinos and a black leather jacket, a diminutive fellow with wavy iron grey hair. He looked a Jewish-Italian criminal, the guy who operates a stolen car ring.

All of a sudden, he stopped talking, moved over to the bed, fixed me with a solemn stare. "Quite seriously my man. I've been watching you from afar."

"Seems to me, you've been watching from close up. This is highly unusual, you know."

"Ah, tsk tsk. That is not worthy of you, such sarcasm and suspicion. You see, you are on that Main Road of which I speak. It is not a well-trod thoroughfare."

"Thanks. And who the hell are you?"

He put his hands on his knees, leaned even closer and spoke slowly, enunciating, "I am Ed Changeling."

He straightened up, did a tap step. "Changeling, get it?"

At that point the door flung open and Bob MacDonald, the guy I shared the apartment with, looked in, his eyes darting worriedly from me to Ed Changeling.

"Yo Bob. This guy here a friend of yours?"

"No, man. I was asleep and heard somebody on the fire escape. Should I call the cops?"

"Hey it's cool," said Ed. "Really, man. You and him and me. All three, we're in it together. Dig? All One. It's fun...it's fun..."

"To be," I mumbled, "part of the Universal One..."

"That's right. I knew it! You are on that path; yes, swimming blithely through the Universal Sea. Pardon the mixing of metaphors or whatever they are. The thing is, my reconnoitering revealed that you have wisdom, which is why I am here."

"Well, since you are here, I suppose you could use some coffee."

"Sure, three sugars."

We adjourned to the kitchen where Ed chain-smoked and told us how he saw God in everything. "And I really mean it."

In the middle of this, Miles arrived. Slow-walking, no-talking Miles. God's relentless wet blanket. Miles was Bob's spiritual mentor. Bob assured me that Miles was the only person who really understood Ouspensky.

"You mean," I said to Bob, "that you don't really understand Ouspensky?"

"That's right. Only Miles does."

"Well if you don't, how do you know that he does?"

Bob gave me his exasperated look.

The two of them used to sit up all night while Miles explained Territorium Organum, or so Bob claimed. For months, the only thing I ever heard Miles say was, "More tea!"

I had been in enough carnivals and around enough carnies to know when the gaff was in. It served Miles well, as guru to a bunch of hippies of a philosophic bent who gave him money. A hippie of a philosophic bent being one who owned tarot cards and thought Carlos Santana added a 'y' to his last name when he wrote the books they taught in university.

Actually, it was this meeting of Ed and Miles that made me think the former might be more than just an aging trespasser. Whereas Miles stood there with his slight smirk of condescension, Ed flitted about like a goofy kid. He was playing. There might be some fun along his path.

When Ed was ready to leave, he declared we must see each other again, and made his exit via the fire escape. I saw him often that summer and fall of 1970, in the park, on the streets, mornings when he woke me up. He began climbing the fire escape earlier and earlier. When it got to 6:30 a.m., I told him to desist. He explained that he sometimes took acid at night with his girlfriend, Leslie and, when he was coming down, needed to get out and talk to someone else.

Gradually, I got to know his story. Up until just a few years before, Ed had been filthy rich in New York. He had a degree in business administration from City College, had worked on Wall Street and gotten into real estate which was where he'd made his big money. He devised "Dial-A-Dinner," an operation that guaranteed to deliver a chicken, steak or ribs dinner anywhere in the five boroughs within 45 minutes or your meal free.

One evening he was in an East Side coffee shop, having just closed a deal, when this good-looking, book-toting girl came in with a book and sat nearby. All suave and charming, Ed sauntered over and asked what she was reading. Rudolf Steiner. She had just come from the R.S. Society meeting and suggested he should attend the next one. Naturally he agreed.

One thing led to another. New ideas and new activities, like smoking marijuana cigarettes. Leslie was a fresh-faced, upper-middle-class kid from Long Island with three years completed at Bryn Mawr. They fell in love, and Ed began to pay less and less attention to business. In late 1965, LSD hit New York, and he paid no further attention at all to business.

The powers-that-be had him declared incompetent to manage his finances, and got rid of him on a small pension. By then,

Ed couldn't have cared less, having forsaken material things. Together Ed and Leslie went north to hang around with Timothy Leary, and eventually they landed in Toronto.

Ed told me that Leslie had dropped acid five times a week every week since 1966. Major-sized hits, too. He only did it twice a week, and sometimes, now, might even skip a week. He had lived long enough to handle acid's onslaught, but Leslie had been totally unprepared. Skinny, with mousey hair, she wore short, faded dresses that displayed heartbreaking stick legs and bruised, knobby knees. She walked the streets, head swivelling, like a tourist just in from the prairies. Leslie was the bane of the supermarket staff at Bloor and Robert streets. She would stake the place out and when the time was right, sneak in, making a beeline for the rows of cereal boxes. She'd caress her favorites, opening and closing her eyes with delight throwing her arms wide and exclaiming in a perfect Marilyn Monroe voice, "Ooooh! Frosty Flakes! Tony the Tiger! Ooooh, I love Shreddies!"

The stock boys and assistant manager soon arrived on the run, closing in on her from both ends of the aisle. They trapped Leslie like a frightened base runner and gave her the heave-ho, laughing as they went. One time, Ed and I happened to arrive on the scene, and he was there to accept her at the automatic doors with tears in his eyes.

Ed wrote his little pantheistic poems, and I published them in an underground paper. The deal between us was that he must not have had them printed elsewhere. He also turned out a play on his big subject, The Universal Sea. He would act the part of the Main Dolphin and me, Dolphin Number Two. We had a ball casting the rest of the fish. Ace Miller, the world's oldest thief, was in it, as well as a retired sea captain who sold newspapers on the street. My pal Marcel Horne, the fire-breather, was the Whale, though he resented the implication. In the middle eighties, I was in Vancouver, going down the alley between Hastings and Pender, near Abbott Street.

There was a guy with a beard in a filthy windbreaker. He was standing on a plastic milk crate going through the Dumpster and he had a baseball glove on each hand. He said hello and I said hello. Then he said, "Oh man. Don't you remember me? I was the Tuna."

After the play, Ed and I had a falling out over a trivial matter. He was double-dealing with his poems, publishing them elsewhere. When I pointed out that he'd sworn not to give me previously published stuff, he got angry, took back everything he had said about my enlightened condition and ducked out the window.

It had been over twenty years, and here he was in a washroom in Kelowna. Taking the pencil, I asked if he remembered those old days.

"Yeah," he said. "They were good times."

"Where you headed?" I scribbled.

He shrugged, "East."

Being conscious of how small his writing pad was and, not wanting to use up any more of it, I patted him on the shoulder, and he patted me on the shoulder and we walked out of there.

I expected he'd duck out the back way but he held his head up and went out through the main room with all the rock and rollers smirking his way, kind of like Miles used to regard him. When he got to the front door, he looked over at me, raised his arms before his chest, and made a gesture like he was doing the breast stroke. It took me a moment to understand. Then he opened the door and was gone, out into the Universal Sea and headed for the highway.

THE MERRY WIDOW

We were at a table in a pub in the Exchange district in Winnipeg. The other guy was a "world famous architect, a local treasure," or at least that's how the woman at the arts magazine had described him.

We'd been to his office where a dozen people were hunched over drawing boards. On the walls were plans for projects in Budapest and Barcelona. In his late forties, making lots of money, dressed in layers of silk, with a tan in Winnipeg in November, the man was a success and not objectionable really. I wanted to like him but it was difficult.

A photo album was open on the table. It was, he stressed, his "personal" photo album. And I realized I was to feel honoured that he was making this generous effort to help me, giving of his time, while Budapest and Barcelona waited. For my part, I was trying not to be annoyed, telling myself there was no way he could possibly benefit from the discussion.

And just as I was convincing myself, he went and showed where the benefit to myself came in.

"There are no really interesting buildings in Manitoba," he said.

"No?"

"But there are two just over the Ontario border. Two that I built. My fishing lodge and my family get-away. Here look. This is my fishing lodge. You see the window that's like a lightning bolt? Do you know why I put that in?"

"Gee, because in that country there is plenty of lightning and you decided to make reference to it?"

He appeared mildly annoyed that I had picked up on it. Hell, I was mildly annoyed that he would consider I wouldn't pick up on it.

"Well, yes. And here you see my family getaway place, walkways thrust into the bush from the second level...."

I was just beginning my search for bizarre homes, yards and gardens. I hadn't seen many as yet, at least not in person, but I knew what I was after. I told the architect about the two places I had seen. One was a house and outbuildings made out of bottles. The other a yard filled with plywood cut-out flowers and plywood cut-out trees.

"That fellow told me he liked flowers but didn't like all the work of gardening, and anyway the weather was bad and the soil was poor. But here he was doing much more work cutting all those flowers out, painting them, varnishing them so they'd stand up to winter. Hundreds of them."

I laughed. The world famous architect just stared at me. He was going to be patient because I was dense after all.

"But all of that is, well, superficial," he said. "There are no ideas behind those kinds of projects. Oh, sure, they may be of some interest in the vernacular but it is mostly people simply fooling around."

"Hey!"

We both looked around for the voice.

"You guys!"

It was a half–native woman sitting by herself a couple of tables away.

"Yeah?" I said.

"She just wants to bum a drink," the architect muttered. "If you speak to her, she's liable to come over."

"I been listening to you," the woman said. She was fat, her face seemed perfectly round, long black hair spilled over the shoulders of her parka. She was all bundled up in the overheated pub.

"You have?" I said.

"Yeah, and I know just the kind of place you want to go and see, buddy."

She fixed her eyes on me.

"Oh, yeah?"

"Just go out onto Main Street there and go until you get to I think it's Washington, or close to it, turn right go four or five blocks. Crazy white lady owns the place."

"What's it like?"

She looked at me for a moment as if considering how to describe the place.

"I don't know how to put it in words, eh? But you'll know it when you see it."

"Thanks."

"Hey, no problem."

She turned her attention to her glass of draft, and I looked back at the architect.

"There's nothing of interest out there," he said. "I can assure you."

After accompanying the architect back to his office and thanking him for his "help" I got in the car and headed out Main Street. My search for weird places would go on for years, is still going on, but had I known then that the persons on this earth least likely to have any appreciation of this kind of thing were architects, my thoughts about this one would have been more tolerant. Architects can't help the way they are.

No one at the convenience store where I stopped knew of any unusual homes in the area. It was getting dark. I drove around the streets for another half hour before giving up and going back to the motel.

The next morning, Saturday, I was about to head north to Cook's Creek to see an ornate Ukranian Catholic church built by a priest named Father Ruh when I decided to make another attempt to find the crazy white lady's place.

I found it.

Paintings and collages were hung all over the outside of the two–story house, the yard was filled with junk and what might not have been junk, as well as what seemed, to me anyway, to be sculpture, and a lady wearing a large red floppy hat, a blue man's bathrobe and pale blue polyester slacks was standing in the middle of it all waving a plastic travel mug of coffee the size of a watering can. She looked like she might have sprouted out of the midst of the rubble.

There were two hand–painted signs in the yard, one close to the street, the other all but lost amid the stuff. They announced "Yard Sale" and "ART".

Well, like the Indian woman had said, I knew it when I saw it.

I parked across the street—turns out it wasn't Washington Street—leaned against the car and surveyed the scene. The front of the house was painted yellow, at least what could be seen of it between the paintings and collages. Some of the paintings were of naked women. Others I couldn't make hide nor hair of, and it probably didn't matter. Most of the sculptures on the lawn consisted of metal bits and plastic bits joined by pieces of wire. One was a tower of plastic pop bottles of all sizes tied to a seven-foot high rusted pipe. At the base of the tower was what looked like a perfectly good vacuum cleaner.

Walking across the street, I got a better look at the daubs of paint on the roof and noticed a rope looped around the chimney, and hanging down over the side of the house. Bleach bottles were attached to the rope and the rope branched out when it reached a second floor window, different bleach bottle branches going off like plastic ivy. There was a young Korean guy poking around in the stuff. It started to snow.

In the middle of the lawn was something made of bedsprings, coathangers, and plumbing pipe partially covered by a dirty white sheet. At the top of the heap were metal blades from hand trowels. Around everything was tied a large pair of woman's underwear.

"Well what do you think it is?"

The woman was at my side. She was large, big bellied, her skin gone pink in the cold.

I looked at the thing and back at her. Snowflakes were settling on her blue bathrobe shoulders.

"The Statue of Liberty," I said. "In her Johnsons."

"Why I'll be fucked," she said. "You're the first person who got it. And I haven't heard the word Johnsons in donkey's years. Those are my Johnsons Miss Liberty is wearing."

They were black and very large. I didn't want to think about it.

"I use panties in a lot of my art. Bras too. Teddys, whatever. I'll show you some of those pieces. I don't keep them out here."

The Korean fellow came over, a small fist full of knives, forks and spoons.

"How much this?"

"I can't talk to you now," the lady said with a brusque gesture of her hand. "Come back in a couple of minutes."

He went away.

"I like you," she said to me. "I bet we could be friends. What's your name?"

I told her and she told me her name was Mary Garmaise.

"But I call myself Merry Garmaise. Because I'm so merry all the time. The merry widow, that's me."

"How come you're so merry, Merry?"

"Cause of that bastard husband of mine. He made me happy

by kicking the bucket. Heart attack. Seven years ago and that's the only time he ever made me happy. I was your average stupid boring typical housewife. Stayed at home and cleaned house. Same house."

She jerked a thumb at the yellow house with the stuff hanging on the wall.

"At first, I wanted to get another place so I wouldn't always be reminded of how miserable I was for forty years. Then I got the idea, like a giant cartoon lightbulb floating over my head, to transform the joint. I wanted to make art, have wanted to make art all my life but never did."

"Husband didn't want you to?"

"The bastard always made fun of me but even before I got married, back when I was a little girl, I had an older sister and she was prettier and she used to draw and my mother and father thought she was wonderful but when I started drawing they told me not to waste my time."

Here came the Korean guy, holding up the kitchen utensils.

"Want to buy. Student."

"You want to buy a student?"

"Yes. Very much."

"Well if another one comes around I'll see what I can do. Boy or girl?"

He looked confused, pointed to himself, "Boy."

"Okay. You come back in five minutes."

The fellow looked disappointed but went over to another part of the lawn, began looking at some old rakes and shovels.

"Where was I? Oh, yes indeed. Miserable all my life. My art inclinations frustrated. Soon as Lloyd was toes up, I enrolled in college to study art. You won't believe it maybe but I got my Masters in Fine Arts. Two years ago that was. Had I led another kind of life, I might consider all of that a waste of time. Art school, I mean. But I'd been isolated, you see and now I was meeting people doing stuff I wanted to do, and it was good for me. Once all that was over with, I really stretched out. I wake up in the morning, have my pot of tea and the rest of the day I do whatever I want to do. I paint, I sculpt, I make collages. What should I call it? I collage-ify? I assemble. In the middle of the day I generally hit the thrift stores and buy old panties, some bras, short sexy teddies—well, maybe they'd be sexy on someone else—but mostly panties. I'm just crazy about panties. How about you?"

"Well, no Merry. At least, not for myself."

"Oh, silly. That's not what I mean. I can tell you're not that type. I mean panties on females. What do you think about that?"

"Sure, Merry. Sexy panties. Yeah, I'm all for them."

"Lacy things?"

"Oh yeah."

"Satiny?"

"Sure."

"How about ones with pictures on them? Like valentines or lips or cute little figures, teddy bears, or something?"

"No, tell you the truth, I don't go for that."

"Same with me. Gee, Jimmy. May I call you Jimmy?"

"Sure thing."

"Thanks. Well it looks like we got a lot in common."

"Sort of, yeah."

"Say, Jimmy. What do you think of the crotchless style of Johnsons?"

Where was the Korean guy when I needed him? I looked, he was over examining a tower of toaster ovens.

"They're fine in theory. Depends on the person wearing them."

"Oh, I agree. I agree. I'm starting to get interested in shoes. The crazier the better. Haven't worn heels for decades. Bought a pair back in the fifties but when I put them on Lloyd called me a slut. They have tremendous potential in art. I made a little car or probably it's more like a truck out of one high heel. Sometimes I wear them around the house at night and other stuff too, lingerie and all."

I didn't say anything to that.

"Hey," she said. "It's just my harmless fantasy. That's another thing I had to stifle when I was married. My fantasies. Forty years. Forty years of fantasy and desire. Killed by dullard husband. No Time to Play Says Insurance Man Tired From Hard Day at Office. How about that for a headline? Or No Time for Sexy Underwear Says Sleepy Underwriter?"

"Want buy!" cried the Korean. "Want buy!"

"Can't you see we're talking about important things here?" Merry said.

The fellow shrugged.

"Go away," she pushed her hands at him. "Get out. Beat it. Scram!"

The Korean fellow just stood there grinning.

"How many ways can I put it?" she looked at me and shrugged.

"How about 'skeedaddle?'" I said.

"Skeedaddle!" she cried. "Take the damned utensils with you."

He didn't understand. I took the stuff from his hands, put the knives and forks and spoons in his parka pocket and waved goodbye. He grabbed my hand, shook it and walked away. I wondered what kind of school he went too.

"I wonder," Merry said. "What kind of fantasies Koreans have?"

"Beats me."

"Well it's getting cold. I better get in the house."

"Been nice knowing you, Merry."

"Oh, no. Jimmy. We have to meet again. You're invited for dinner. Tonight. What do you say? I'll show you all my work."

The snow didn't increase so I drove north toward Cook's Creek, and forty-five minutes later saw the huge Ukranian Catholic

Church rise out of the flat land. It was painted a yellowy-sand colour with blue trim and daubed all over with white paint. Inside were murals, African-like painting touches and fake palm trees. I learned that old Father Ruh never had any architectural or construction training, just built churches where they were needed. Thirty or more over the prairies and down into the States. He could cure sickness by the laying on of hands. But that's another story.

Back at the motel in town, there was enough time to have a shower and change. The old lady was funny and so was her artwork. I felt sure she knew lots of people casually but few of them would want to get too close, thinking she was nuts. She was but so what?

When she opened the sidedoor, the kitchen door, at seven-thirty I was pleased to see that she was wearing a moo-moo and her old bathrobe. While parking the car, I'd had this vision of her greeting me in some frayed and mismatched lingerie ensemble from a Cyclopean crossdresser's thrift store, her lips smeared with bright red lipstick, feet like hams in stiletto heels. But she looked the same as she had in the afternoon, except she'd run a brush through her thick grey hair.

The old-fashioned kitchen smelled good. There were four covered pots on the stove.

"So glad you came. I was afraid you might wimp out. Dinner with an old hag, you crazy? Ha, ha!" she laughed and took the bottle of merlot that I held out.

"I hope you like venison."

Venison? I'd feared something out of a can, remembering the time I'd had dinner at an albino artist's home in Melbourne. Canned goat stew, canned stringbeans and canned baby onions she'd served on paper plates. With grape juice. But the woman could really draw.

She took off her bathrobe and hung it over her chair. There were half a dozen colours to her moo-moo but orange was dominate.

"Sit, please. It's ready now. I'll show you my art later. There's a bottle of pinot noir on the table that's opened. Why don't we drink that first and your bottle later. I also have a Cabernet Sauvignon on the counter there. You pour, me serve."

Venison, wild rice, asparagus, a salad of endive and shredded beets. She'd carefully spooned just enough gravy on top of the venison that it trickled over the side. The gravy had a lemony wine taste to it. Everything was delicious. I told her so as we clicked glasses.

"That bastard. You know who I mean. He was strictly a beef and potatoes kind of guy. Once, and once only, I made rice. When he sees it, he says, 'What do you think, I've turned chink?' He was just so goddamned cosmopolitan. The slob."

He left her the house, a few thousand dollars, and a lot in the north end that she sold. What with that and her old age pension, she didn't have to worry. Could devote all her time to making her art. The kitchen walls held collages. But the "good stuff" was in the other rooms.

We talked about a little of everything but mostly about art. She didn't care much for most of the pooh bahs of Canadian art, particularly the Group of Seven.

"I'm with you there, Merry."

"And Christopher Pratt. I mean, give me a break."

"I hear you."

"Bertram Bining was okay though imitating stuff from elsewhere."

"Yeah, too bad he had that job."

We were into the second bottle of wine.

"I like that fellow Morrice," she said.

"Yeah, me too. And there's the guy in Ontario who just died. From St. Thomas. Clark MacDougall."

"He the one who does street scenes that always look glossy, like they've been highly varnished?"

"Yeah, that's him."

"He's really good," Merry agreed. "But I'd trade any of those people for that old lady from Nova Scotia. But she was lucky. Her husband let her make art. Hell, he didn't mind if she painted the walls or the goddamned bread box."

When we'd finished the wine, she poured us glasses of Cointreau. "Come on I'll show you some of my stuff."

The livingroom walls were covered with art, so was the hallway, and the walls in the bathroom. She must have done a hundred paintings of items of female under apparel. You'd see a big high heel shoe and a little man or woman standing beside it. A group of people taking shelter from a storm under a pair of panties. A party of trekkers scaling both cups of a brassiere.

While I looked at all of this, she retrieved the Cointreau from the kitchen and filled our glasses. "These are just my fantasies, like I told you before. Nothing wrong with that, is there?"

"Not at all, Merry."

"There's something else."

Before I could say "What's that?" she had the moo moo most of the way up her body. The thing got caught on her breasts which a couple of seconds later I could compare to manatees. During the interim I got to see her very large legs, black stockinged three quarters of the way up and, above that, all fish belly white and parcelled into sections by garter straps, like quarter sections in snow.

And just above that I didn't dare look.

"Shit!" she exclaimed, yanking the moo moo the rest of the way.

I had been speechless with surprise during the undressing but finally I managed an "Uggh."

She stood there before me big and white and old.

White except for her face that had gone a deep pink.

"Well at least you haven't run away. Yet."

I was thinking about it.

"Listen," she said, as if to cut off my retreat. "What's the harm in it? Really. I'm just doing what I do most every night. Dress up in sexy stuff. Well, I feel sexy in it. The only difference is, I got company. It's thrilling having you here just looking at me. It's not like I'm asking you to do anything, is it?"

"No."

"I mean if you wanted to do something that would be great. I haven't had anything done to me for twenty years. I don't imagine you would, though."

"That's right, Merry. I'm not going to do anything."

"Oh, well. You want me to do something to you? I will."

"Uh, no thanks."

"Okay. I won't say another word about it. Nor make any allusion. I bet you need another drink though, eh?"

"I sure do."

She laughed. Poured me one, handed it to me, emptied the bottle into her glass and carried it with her to the couch. It was quite a sight. I looked away, down at the old carpet. I felt rooted to the spot, the middle of her livingroom. I considered the options. If I bolted, she'd just feel embarrassed and humiliated. She's just a crazy old lady, what the hell.

When I looked up Merry was sitting on the couch with her legs spread. When she reached down I realized the blue satin panties were crotcheless. She began to tickle herself with the middle finger of her right hand. She looked up and giggled.

"You just do what you're doing," she said. "Don't go anywhere. Just stay in the room."

She took the cointreau bottle, and put it between her legs. The lip of it was poised at the lips of her vagina. She held it there. "What does this look like?" she asked me.

"It looks like you're going to give it a drink."

She laughed, and eased the neck into her. Pushed it in further.

"That feels good," she said.

Merry began moving on it. On the thick part of the bottle. The damn thing looked like it was going to disappear inside her.

She'd glance at me, then up at the ceiling and back again. I turned away, walked around the room while she was working. She had painted an old tv set and on top of the set was a block of clear plastic, like a block of ice, in which was suspended a small garter belt, The little belts hung down and there were little lead fishing line weights at the bottoms. At the middle of the block, near the bottom were two little plastic men in tuxedos, the grooms usually found on the top of wedding cakes.

"Uhggh! Marine...Uhggh!"

I turned. She was looking at me. Her face all pink again.

"Marine fibreglass! Ooooh. Uhggh! Expensive. Won't be long now!"

She took one hand off the bottle, and groped inside her bra, pulled out one manatee breast and squeezed the brown spreading nipple, while ramming the bottle inside her with the other hand. I looked away and after a few seconds going at it frantically, Merry hollered, sputtered, groaned and finally screamed.

I glanced at the door, thinking of the neighbors bursting in and looked back just in time to see the Cointreau bottle pop out like a little brown baby.

Her arms fell to her sides. She lay back panting, heaving's more like it. I was put in mind of a beached whale stranded on shore tangled in a Brobdingnagian goddess's underthings.

Was she going to have a heart attack? If so, what should I do? Undress her before the ambulance arrived? Get the moo-moo on her?

She moaned. Opened an eye. Opened the other. Turned them on me. Took deep breaths. "Oooohh!" she murmured. "Thanks for that."

"You're welcome," I said. "Nothing to it."

"Oh, Lord. It was great! It hasn't happened for a couple of years. Wow! I try practically every night. Sometimes I get real close. Right to the edge but never over. Thank you, thank you. You can have anything you want. Anything."

"I don't want anything, don't be silly."

"You want money? There's an old car in the garage out back. It's yours."

"That's okay. I better be going now, Merry."

"Oh, no. Why don't you stay and I'll try for seconds."

"I have to go."

"Ah, you won't be back will you?"

"Got to leave town tomorrow. Head west."

"It's been nice knowing you. You're always welcome."

I got my coat, gave her a little wave. She was still slumped on the couch. She picked up the cointreau bottle and waved it at me.

"Have a drink of this sometime and think of Merry the widow."

AT LARGE

Reports had indicated that a good part of the river was navigable up to the foot of the cordillera. It isn't, of course.
Alvaro Mutis

RHODESIA —

LAST OF THE NINTH

The crimson sun was a ragged gash across the bottom of a big African sky and looked about to bleed over the centerfield fence. A mercenary from Minnesota was playing third and the pitcher was a Matabele tribesman. The former had his eyes on the batter but the latter darted me a nervous, over–the–shoulder glance as I took another step away from second base. When he looked to the plate and lifted his cleated foot from the rubber, I was off.

Settling into an aisle seat, I recognized my neighbour from the airport lounge in Johannesburg, a compact man with close-cropped, carrot-coloured hair and a nose that was so small it almost seemed apologetic. He had an attaché case on his thighs and was making checkmarks on sheets of paper. When we were ready for takeoff, he snapped shut the case, stowed it under the seat, folded his stubby freckled hands, and stared straight ahead.

Only when we were in the air and levelled off did he relax.

"Will it be your first time in Rhodesia?" he asked, turning to me.

I told him it was, and that I had just spent three weeks in South Africa.

"Please do not judge us by them. People make that mistake. Mostly it is the fault of those damned journalists."

"Well that's what I am, a journalist. Damned too, probably."

He gave me a measuring look before advising that people in the two countries were quite different. "And the difference is easy enough to discern should anyone care to look."

The line was probably meant as a dismissal and maybe even a warning.

When the man took off his sportcoat, I noticed the emblem on his dark green sweatshirt; it was handsewn and comprised of two baseball bats crossed over a prominent letter 'S.'

"Baseball?" I said, "I thought this was cricket country."

I wanted to show him that although a journalist, I was not without everyday interests.

"Maybe in the rest of Africa. Baseball has caught on big in Rhodesia. We have professional ball. In fact, I've been in Johannesburg picking up a shipment of gloves and bats from America. They don't trade with us directly, of course. I'm the manager of the Salisbury team, the Sultans."

His name was Eric Whitten. By introducing himself, I supposed he was acknowledging the possibility that I might be a decent individual after all. He wanted to know if I had ever played baseball. Up there, ten thousand metres above the troubled land, I recalled riding the bus alone at age twelve, with a change of clothes, a pair of spikes and Wilson A2000 glove, across Pennsylvania to the home of a Pittsburgh Pirate scout in Morganton, West Virginia.

"You ever hear of the Pittsburgh Pirates?"

"Certainly," he said. "Dave Parker."

The military was very much in evidence at the Salisbury airport. Whitten and I sat together on the bus into town. Eucalyptus trees twisted out of the sandy soil and it all looked exactly like my idea of Africa. There had been an attack on an airport bus in the past month. The man kept talking baseball and I kept watching the woods for lions and guerillas.

The Meikles Hotel was my stop. Whitten owned the sporting goods store a couple of blocks away on the other side of the plaza. "Come by and we can talk. The second part of the season begins in a couple of days."

I went into the Meikles. There was a tall, no-nonsense middle–aged woman at the desk by a sign that read: "Check All Guns Here."

When I had filled out the card, she said, "May I see to your guns, sir?"

"Don't have a single one."

Her expression left it unclear whether she thought I was a nut or a subversive.

"Journalist," I said. "Against international rules, you see."

I took a turn around town before dinner, and to my unfocused eye it was difficult to believe this was the capital of a country at war. Blacks and whites read newspapers on benches in the plaza. There were posters advertising sales, a prize fight, discos. People came out of boutiques with plastic, chocolate-coloured shopping bags. They sat at tube-and-formica tables on the mall eating salads and hamburgers with silly names. The camps of blacks in the market square, blacks who had fled their villages for fear of terrorist attack, might have been set down in Savannah, Georgia. The Woolworth's on the plaza had been bombed a couple of months ago but it was open for business now.

That night I put in an appearance at several pubs because I figured it was my responsibility, being a foreign correspondent and all that. There was "the mood of the people," to be discovered. Besides I would have gone to the pubs anyway. Turned out the pubs were just about the best places to go to avoid journalists. The only place where you stood less chance of encountering one was at the front. I soon learned how the big deal foreign correspondents worked. After a leisurely breakfast, they ventured over to the Ministry of Information at ten o'clock to receive the government line from a Colonel Gates. The handouts were taken back to the hotel lobby and ridiculed over the day's first drinks. They deserved to be ridiculed but, as well, they were reinterpreted through the perspective of various contacts the correspondents cultivated. Every correspondent professed to have important "contacts" within the guerilla movements. These were often the black waiters in starched white smocks who served drinks in Meikles. Each waiter had a brother-in-law or knew somebody else who was a close friend of somebody who was a guerrilla, and these became, to readers in London and New York, "a source close to Robert Mugabe" or "a reliable figure within the guerilla movement."

After lunch, the correspondents retired to their rooms to write their stories or take naps or whatever else they did up there, and appeared again for drinks in the late afternoon.

Anyway, at the third or fourth pub, a fellow bought me a beer and invited me to celebrate with him. He had that very afternoon completed his annual stint of military service. He was not, however, a callow youth, an observation I tried to express as diplomatically as possible. "I'm forty-bloody-eight years old!" he exclaimed, his face flushed by sun and booze. "And I'm obliged to serve for six more years. God willing. And this makes me no different than any other white male in the country. Blacks are excluded from conscription but may enlist."

His khaki shirt was opened to where his belly began to swell. He talked about patrolling the bush and how intense the heat could become. "You're out there marching under all that gear, no longer a young man, the sweat rolls down into your eyes, the belt is chaffing your skin, you stumble right into a branch that cuts your bloody forehead and you want to cry out in frustration, want to just give up the whole show because who cares."

I told him I was interested in going to the front.

"All right, mate," says he. "I'll take you."

After downing another pint, he asked me if I was ready.

"Ready to go to the front?"

"Right now?"

"Yes. Why delay?"

"Well, I ought to go back to Meikles and fetch my gear."

"What's the matter with the way you are?"

"Might need some other stuff and, anyway, perhaps I should check out of the hotel."

"Good lord, man. Where do you think the front is?"

"Hell if I know. Twenty? Thirty miles away?"

"No, it's around my house. The suburbs. Five minute drive at most. Come now. Let's be off. Hip, hip. To the front!"

After parking near his house but not right in front of his house, the man took a handgun from the glove box, pushed in a clip, and advised me to follow in his footsteps.

We walked a crooked path across the lawn to his door, me directly in back of him wondering if he wasn't having his little joke at my expense. I thought back to living in the Yukon, the old timers funning cheechakos. Later I realized he wasn't kidding.

I met his wife, her brother, their teenaged son. A Ridgeback dog lay under the kitchen table, stolid but alert. Two rifles leaned against the wall and in a cupboard over the sink were half a dozen mines that reminded me of small curling rocks.

They informed me that in this district everyone's yard was mined and that there was a skirmish every few nights.

While they reminisced about neighborhood battles, I noticed the pattern of the wallpaper—Dutch men and Dutch women in wooden shoes, windmills, tulips. There were fingerprints around the light switch. Under the wall phone was a metal tv tray that held an address book, a little wooden box with file card recipes and a South American Lama machine pistol.

We talked around the table until dawn when the man drove me back to town and let me out in front of the hotel.

There was a knot of people at the reception desk gathered round a short wave radio. From the way they looked up at me, I knew they were listening to bad news. It was as if they were silently inviting me to join their uncomprehending circle.

Terrorists had massacred the white teachers and their children at the Emmanuel Mission School southeast of the town of Umtali. The announcer said there were probably thirteen dead but that it was difficult to know for certain because the bodies had been so badly mutilated.

"Where is Umtali?"

"Mountains of the Mist area," someone told me.

"In the east highlands," said another. "Close to the Mozambique border."

The ground in front of the goalie's net on the soccer field at the Emmanuel School was still wet with blood. There were trails of blood through the grass surrounding the buildings. Bodies or the remains of bodies were covered with tarpaulin. Security police foraged for human limbs in the shrubbery.

The students, all black, said that during the night, men claiming to be from Robert Mugabe's ZANLA, the armed branch of the Zimbabwe African National Union, had entered the dormitories, woken the students, and announced themselves. They carried Russian Kalashnikov rifles and machetes. After delivering a political explanation of what they were going to do, the guerillas rounded up the missionaries and their children and took them to the playing field. The men were slaughtered last. They and the children were made to watch as the four women were raped repeatedly before being butchered. The children were killed with knives. The men saw this before they were hacked to death.

Later, from his headquarters in Mozambique, Mugabe

claimed he had nothing to do with the massacre and declared that the black killers were actually members of the Rhodesian Army.

After three hours, I left the school and began hiking to town along a road like a rope flung down on long grass that glittered in the weak sunlight and trembled at every breeze. This was the countryside celebrated by the great white hunter Frederick Selous, whose name was appropriated by the elite corps of the Rhodesian forces. After I had walked a mile or so, an army truck pulled over and a bald man leaned down to ask me who the hell I was and what the hell I was doing.

"There's a war going on out there, sport."

He drove me into Umtali where I stayed over at a lodge near the train station. The main street was lined with cherry trees and it must have been pretty when they were in blossom. Mountains were all around and any white resident was pleased to point out the way the settlers had come, just over there through Christmas Pass.

It was here in Umtali, in 1911, that the Constitutional Crisis occurred. An African named Alukuleta was found guilty of rape and sentenced to death but the High Commissioner, Lord Gladstone, overturned the decision and had the man freed, an action that nearly brought down the government.

The next day I met a young black soldier named Philomon who offered me a ride to Salisbury. He said it would be a slow trip because of the afternoon curfew.

We started off immediately in his Ford Anglia. Philomon was short and wiry, dressed in camouflage suit and floppy hat. Around his waist was a perforated belt that held a holster and pistol. As we drove, Philomon told me how he became a soldier. He had attended a missionary school like the one I'd just left, and had been an eager student and star soccer player. His dream, which seemed an impossibility, had been to go to university. One day some men came to see him at his home in Gwelo.

"All I knew was that they were interested in politics. They said they had a scholarship for me so that I could attend university in Canada. There would be no expense to me or my family for anything. These men had also taken care of all papers and visas. We were to leave soon. At the appointed date, an escort came for me and we flew to Nairobi and changed to another plane, and went to some other place, and changed planes again. Five times we changed planes..."

He never saw Canada. When Philomon got off the last plane, he was in East Germany. "I spent a year at a school there and learned the Russian language and about Marxism. I also had courses in communications, weaponry and such things as techniques of explosives, poisons, ciphers and codes—they're not the same thing. Even the psychology of torture. It was good training."

Next he was delivered to Moscow and spent six months at the Patrice Lamumba Institute.

After his year and a half, Philomon was returned to Africa and dropped by helicopter into Mozambique. He crossed the border into Rhodesia, near Chipinga, and was given the responsibility of organizing a small cell of recruits to operate in the area, raiding farms and blowing up bridges as whites crossed in their cars. A fifteen year old kid was chosen to be his assistant.

"The boy told me he had been promised a good job, a car and plenty of white women once the Party took over in Zimbabwe.

"One day we were camped near the ruins at Chibyumani. I told them to wait for me, that I was going to stop a car, rob the driver and go to find supplies. I did stop a car but it was to ask for a ride into Fort Victoria. There I joined the Rhodesian Army."

We passed the town of Odzi and were in the Mtanda Mountains. The Anglia strained as it climbed a long hill. On the horizon, a few miles off we saw a truck top the rise, then two more trucks, all of them shimmering in the heat.

"They will probably stop to warn us...."

Several shots hit our car like a line of period marks. They came from the right, the driver's side, and Philomon swerved the

Anglia the other way. A bullet shattered his window and went through the roof a few inches behind my head. Before we bumped to a stop on the dirt shoulder, I had gotten the door open and tumbled out on the ground. Philomon, grabbing for his pistol, came out on top of me, rolled off and began firing blindly into the bush on the other side of the road.

More shots hit the car and it was a long couple of minutes before the Army vehicles arrived on the scene. Peeking from behind the front tire of the Anglia, I made out two vague forms in the bush on the other side of the road. Then I saw one of the guerrillas clearly. He was carrying a sten gun—I remember thinking how flimsy it seemed—and wearing a red beret, black t-shirt, and black and white high topped sneakers.

Half a dozen soldiers hit the road running. Two crashed into the brush and the others fired short bursts from submachine guns with drilled chrome barrels. Smoke spilled from the holes and hung in the late afternoon air.

I lay there in the dirt listening to the gunfire and picking bits of thick glass from my hair. The edges of the glass were worn smooth like pieces you'd find on the beach. I felt curiously detached from it all, and calm.

After several minutes the firing diminished. There were a few more desultory exchanges and finally the shooting ceased.

"They weren't after us," Philomon concluded. "They knew the Army would be by on curfew patrol and that they'd have to gear down coming over the hill."

And we must have seemed like a bonus.

The first soldier emerged from the woods and came over to us.

"There were five of them," he said. "We got one anyway."

Later, I shook hands with each of the soldiers and thanked them. Most were white, a few black. They lifted the body of the dead man onto the back of the truck. They asked if I was American and seemed pleased when I told them I was Canadian. One soldier sort of looked me over, nodded and said, "We're about the same size."

He went to a truck and brought back an olive green Selous Scout t-shirt from his kit.

"Just a souvenir of your visit to Rhodesia," he smiled. "And don't worry, mate. It's clean."

Back in the capitol two days later, I looked up Eric Whitten, the guy I'd met on the plane. Over lunch, he gave me the news about his baseball club, the Sultans, and invited me to the game that evening.

It could have been a park in the lower minor leagues in a long-gone America. The grass was rough but freshly cut, infield dirt the colour of rust, foul lines white as snow, if a little uncertain. I thought to myself that the businesses advertised on the outfield fences probably didn't sign up for the long-term rates.

Whitten was in a partitioned area under the bleachers that served as a clubhouse. The players, both colours, were putting on their uniforms. "Why don't you take batting practice with us," he said casually.

"Come on, I haven't swung a bat since I was a kid."

"Well, you just hold the thing down near the bottom, in case you've forgotten, one hand on top of the other."

He insisted I put on a uniform. At first I felt awkward. But the scrape of the cleats on concrete was familiar.

The rest of the team was out on the field. Two black players stood by the cage talking. The other team, the Cowboys, from Bulawayo, had taken their cuts and, walking single file toward the clubhouse, made me think of cows heading for the barn. I stood behind the cage watching the ball come in. When the rest of them had hit, Whitten gave me the nod.

I topped the first pitch into the dirt in front of me, missed the next two, and directed a shame-faced look at Whitten who glanced away. I felt exactly like a middle-aged idiot whose fantasy had just been whiffed by reality. But then I hit a sharp grounder and looked at things differently. The last pitch, I tagged deep into the outfield.

"Thanks," I told Whitten, stepping out of the box. "That was fun."

"What position did you used to play?"

"First base, third base."

"Go down to third and take some grounders."

Twenty minutes later, back in the clubhouse, I was pulling off the jersey when Whitten said, "Stay dressed, might be able to use you."

"You're kidding."

"Hardly. Tough group, this Bulawayo bunch. Might need your help."

The Salisbury Sultans took the field and I sat on the bench with six other guys. Whitten ignored us like a manager anywhere. The Cowboys scored two runs in the first; the Sultans caught up in the fourth and went ahead by a run. The opposing pitcher had a fast ball that didn't hop, a curve that didn't drop and a lousy move to first. The catcher's arm wasn't bad but one of our guys, the second baseman, a black kid with three scars on each cheek who couldn't have been twenty, stole second standing up.

When the Cowboys were retired at the top of the seventh, the score stood at six–five, Sultans. Whitten leaned forward down at his end of the bench. "You're hitting for the pitcher," he called to me. "Get out to the on-deck circle."

"Me?"

"Yeah, you."

He wrote on his lineup card.

My legs actually began to tremble, something they hadn't done on the road out of Umtali, and I had to pause before attempting the dugout steps.

"Get going!"

Grabbing a bat, I hurried to the circle and busied myself with swings and stretches to hide my nervousness. The hitter bounced the first pitch to second for an easy out and all too soon it was my turn.

I hoped at least to get wood on the ball and not embarrass myself. The first pitch was a fastball that I looked at, strike one. The second, outside for a ball. No more fooling around, I'd swing no matter what.

It was intended to be a curve ball but it hung there on the outside of the plate. A gift. I connected and took off running, not knowing if it was fair or foul, and I didn't look up until, almost to first base, I saw the ball skipping along the left field line like a flat stone on still water and headed for the corner. I had myself a standup double.

Standing on the bag, looking around, at the other players, the scattering of fans, the clear sky, the old baseball thing came back to me. It was like my long lost favorite uncle tapping me on the back.

As a kid, like most kids then, I'd wanted to be a professional ball player. Then around age twelve, I'd stopped wanting it, turned to others things and forgot all about baseball.

And here I was twenty years later. It was a league I'd never imagined but it was pro ball of a kind, which made me a professional baseball player of a sort.

Well my earliest hero had been Ty Cobb, and I was in a perfect Ty Cobb situation. One out, last of the eighth, the Sultans needing an insurance run. If the pitcher had a poor move to first, he certainly wasn't about to try second. A right-handed batter was up which would hinder the catcher's throw to third.

The pitcher glanced over nervously as I increased my lead. The third baseman was concentrating on the plate. The pitcher started his move and I was gone. I fell away in a big, classic hook slide. Safe.

As I was brushing the dirt from my pants, the third baseman told me he was from St. Paul. "You patrolling for the Cattleman's

Association?" he asked. "Or are you one of Mike Hoare's people?"

When I winked in reply, he nodded his head conspiratorially.

A minute later I scored on an outfield fly and was greeted with handshakes and slaps on the back from my teammates.

Whitten sent me out to third for the top of the ninth. I handled a routine grounder without throwing the ball away.

After the game, the manager invited me for a drink at Meikles. We sat in the lobby with gin and tonics brought to us by reliable sources. Whitten handed me fifty dollars. "Now you can buy the next round. It's twenty–five when we lose. That is to create incentive. Blacks paid the same as whites in case anyone asks you back home. But I am hoping you won't be going back home just yet."

"What'd you mean?"

"Stay and sign a contract with the Sultans."

"C'mon, I'm thirty–two years old."

"I don't care how old you are. I'm serious. We lose a lot of men because of conscription. It's getting tighter. They just passed a law last year that men my age have to go for ten weeks a year. I can arrange everything with Immigration. Your work permit and such. You can retain your status as a journalist and avoid the draft."

I muttered something about having some experience along those particular lines but he didn't seem to catch my drift.

"When I'm doing my stint, you could take over as manager. You know the game and you're mature. We play split seasons. There are no politics in the league. Fifty games with two months in between. What I can offer you is one hundred dollars a game, enough to live on probably, especially if you do something on the side, public relations perhaps. Don't give me an answer now unless it is yes. Think about it but not for too long. We're going on a road trip day after tomorrow."

While we talked, the international media people milled about the lobby, having arrived to cover the funerals at Umtali. Video equipment and aluminum suitcases were all over the place. A man from Rome in a shortsleeved safari outfit, precise little beard and moustache, called to a willowly blonde American television woman, "Darlinghissima, it has been too long!"

"The Evacuation, right?"

She meant Saigon.

"Your bunch?" Whitten asked me.

"No, not my bunch."

The next morning I read the paper over breakfast. There had been another massacre, this time of blacks. Seventeen people. Ignoring warnings from the guerillas, they had persisted in sending their children to school. Education was for whites, and blacks who supported it were labelled "Tshombes."

Wandering around town, I considered Whitten's offer. I would actually have something resembling a salary for the first time in years. Also, I would be able to dine out on the experience for the rest of my life. "And then there was the time I was player–manager of the Salisbury Sultans. Play was often interrupted by mortar fire but, nevertheless..."

Either that or somebody back in Toronto would answer the question, "Whatever happened to Christy?"— with "Way I understand it, he slid into a landmine disguised as second base in Bulawayo and that was that. Went to pieces you might say."

Out on the boulevard in the afternoon, I sat on the plinth at the feet of Cecil Rhodes, wondering how long he would be there surveying the scene.

Later I went to a movie — of all things "The Betsy" with Laurence Olivier — and came out at twilight. Across the street people were gathered at a used car lot looking over ten year old vehicles with surreal price tags. The last shoppers of the day were hurrying home to Rotten Row.

All these people going about their business as if it was going to last. Every day there were new signs in the windows of vacant shops, "Going back to Britain."

Many who stayed, pretended that things would work out

because they were decent people, different from South Africans. Then there were others who pretended they would prevail because they were white.

There was not a big future for third basemen in Rhodesia. I had to laugh to keep from crying. I telephoned Whitten and told him I had to decline his most generous offer.

"But I was so sure of you, I made out the contract."

"Well, I think before too long, Mr. Mugabe would cancel it."

"Come now, mate."

"Eric, there isn't going to be any Salisbury Sultans in a little while. You must see that."

There was silence for a moment during which I thought he was preparing to tell me off for my presumptuousness which he had every right to do. Instead, he said, "Yes, I suppose I can see that perfectly clearly. This is my country, however, and I love it."

I heard him sigh heavily, "And we must go on, mustn't we?"

"I suppose so."

"Well we take off tomorrow. Offer's still open should you change your mind. If not, cheerio!"

"Yeah, man. Cheerio!"

The next morning the Salisbury Sultans boarded their bus for Fort Victoria and in the evening I caught the plane to begin my own long trip home.

IN SEARCH OF

THE GOLDEN MADONNA

If Geraldo was just a little bit smarter, I would be three months dead.

Home now, a few thousand miles away from the evil slough of Honduras, the original banana republic, I can watch the whole thing like it was a movie—sort of Wages of Fear cast by some omnipotent and evil mestizo bandito who has used only the sick of mind and body, whether home boys from the local streets and rollerboards or imported characters glowing with righteousness from God's country — bad actors all of them. And in the midst of them in the torrid hell-hole, those who are searching for the heathen to be saved, the Commie to be machine-gunned and doused with quick lime, or just searching for a scrap to eat, is myself; I was searching for a billion dollars worth of gold.

The frames click through the gates of memory: escaping the city, the road, the long hike across the cattle fields and into the jungle, fording the angry river, then the slow climb along the slopes of the mountain to the places where the money was hidden. And all that

138

only part of the adventure.

I was midway across a skinny tree trunk that arched over the river, the menacing rocks thirty feet below, at the exact moment my brain stirred from its tropical torpor and I understood that this man wanted to kill me. Reaching the other side, there was nothing to do but wait for him to make his move. I couldn't flee, it was his jungle after all. So I followed, watching his broad back and the furrows in his dark neck. As we marched I thought of all manner of things, none particularly solemn, and I felt very much alive.

One of those particularly solemn things I was thinking as we marched along was that I had his photograph. Before entering into the jungle, I had snapped his picture, a photograph of a guy who, if he was smarter, would be my murderer.

There is a library in the beautiful colonial town of Antigua, Guatemala that is devoted to all aspects of Latin American study, and it was there I came across the only substantial material devoted to the fabled treasure of San Jorge de Olancho and the Golden Madonna; this despite the fact that I had foraged in a dozen other libraries elsewhere and utilized the resources of various computer information banks. The most recent reference to the treasure I was after occurs in a book published in the middle of the last century. Its author was warned by the locals in these very same parts, western Honduras near the Nicaraguan border, to forget about venturing to the buried town for there was a curse upon it. The author had a guide, maybe an ancestor of my Geraldo, who advised, "It is a place shunned by the virtuous and well-disposed, and I should be unwilling to incur the fate of numerous persons who are said to have perished by a similar exhibition of ill-judged curiosity."

The airport at Teguciagalpa, the capital of Honduras, looks like a decrepit tool shed, or a place in New Jersey where Mob underlings come by night to drop off truck loads of nuclear waste. Only a few people got off the flight from Salvador, the rest stayed put, bound for Costa Rica. Inside the place was worse, dimly lit, the veneer peeling from walls, brutal-faced young men with antiquated but deadly guns.

You had to approach a sort of raised plywood and glass box to show your passport to a brown-skinned official who looked like a teenager with aging disease. The glass on the left side of the booth was broken half way up. On his flank stood another guy talking with him. He had a gun and a walkie-talkie at his waist and a face that reminded me of Ishmael on Queequeg: "His countenance was a crucifixion to behold."

The right side of it appeared to have been systematically worked over by a straight razor. This had not been an accident for the left side was completely unmarked. There were at least a hundred cuts and they stopped along the bridge of his nose and at the middle of his forehead; there was a half-moon gouge taken out of his chin with the points of it not straying over an imaginary line drawn vertically down from his lip.

From my position near the end of a line of five, I was able to determine that this man's function, ostensibly, was to assist foreigners. In reality, he discussed them and made fun of them with the customs official. The first four were Americans, all religious workers, and none spoke Spanish. A lady from Ohio asked how she could get to a certain part of town where she wished to visit a minister friend from the States. Before answering her, he explained for the benefit of his partner that the old bitch wanted to see some stupid Protestant, and he went on to describe a couple of aged individuals in the process of making the beast with two backs.

During Easter week in forlorn Tegucigalpa about the only place to get a meal is the Honduran Mayan Hotel, operated by Holiday Inn, and booked solid with American missionaries and American military personnel. These indeed are a bad string of days for the former, the holiest of semanas in a thoroughly Catholic country. They commandeered the coffee shop and lounged poolside with bibles and concordances, staring out over the raggedy Tegu skyline and the tin and cardboard barrios on the bare hillsides, plotting strategies in southern accents. What to do in the face of all this ritual, how to cleanse an atmosphere made sticky with blood and gaudy with death.

"If the Lord will only open His eyes to it. . . ." says an earnest young man at the next table by way of a heartland Four-H Club.

"If we pray to him. . ." replies his mate, an older fellow with teased and sprayed peach-tinted hair.

Business is always booming for the other sort of guest at the Honduran Mayan and he has a more empirical solution: "Military exercises designed solely for the purpose of providing means for the peace-loving Honduran populace to protect themselves from the Communist-dominated, illegal government of Nicaragua."

Translated, what this means is that the policies of the Honduran government are dictated by the United States and should Honduras dare to demur and not allow itself to serve as a base for fighting the Sandinistas, then the U.S.A. will take away the foreign aid that props the country up. The end result: they'll be left hanging on the line with poor Guatemala who said enough is enough and was left with a measly three million dollars — the global version of the nickel tip.

This is not leftist interpretation but a paraphrase of the situation by the resident Company man at the Mayan. The CIA fellow who appeared harmless enough, like a stockbroker or retired baseball player, explained that Honduras would not rebel, never fear; it had always been in this position. Witness the position of the United Fruit Company. "If the countries of Central America were all the guys in the shower in a prison and Uncle Sam was the warden, Honduras would be the guy picking up the soap," he explained.

This, then, is the setting for my search for the legendary site of the fabulous buried city and its nine hundred pound golden madonna.

A year or so earlier, my investigation into Central American antiquities lead me to this, the most romantic of all buried treasure tales. In ancient times in Honduras there existed at the foot of a mountain, a town whose inhabitants used gold in all aspects of their lives. Being the only metal available, it was made into tools, utensils implements of all kinds. Because it was pretty and it glittered, gold was fashioned into jewelry and works of art.

The Spaniards heard of this town and after many years of searching, found the golden city and immediately put the Indians to work mining more gold. The priests came and demanded the rich conquistadors pay a tax of gold which they justified by melting it down and forming into a golden madonna. Finally the pious marauders refused to be tithed anymore and the madonna was without its final touch, the crowning touch, a golden crown. The gentry had the gall to present the priests with a corona de cuerpo, a crown of horsehide. Immediately, as if in response to a sacrilege, the side of the mountain fell away, burying the town that had come to be called San Jorge de Olancho, or Olancho de Viejo. The few survivors fled and re-established themselves elsewhere.

Of course, being a collector of this kind of lore, I knew plenty of treasure trove tales. I even came across two people in Calgary, a gemologist and a geologist, who claimed to have actually visited San Jorge. But if I wanted to throw aside loved ones and the workaday world and go searching for the "X" that marks the spot, there were plenty of places to poke around that were closer to home.

Nevertheless, there was something about the Golden Madonna that nagged at me. It was the most fabulous of stories because, well, because no matter how far-fetched it might appear, there were details that seemed like they could be readily verified or repudiated. And this I set out to do. I had more than the bug, you understand—I had the hunch.

Although no town named San Jorge de Olancho or Olancho de Viejo exists now, if it ever had existed and been so rich and important, then surely, I reasoned, there would be some historical trace. If not, I would cease my inquiries. Had there been gold, the conquistadors would have gone after it for that was half of their mandate — and they would have left records. I would get at them even if it meant going to the archives of Seville. In order to locate the site of the town, I had to affirm the existence of the mountain that protected and eventually destroyed San Jorge.

The earliest mention of what would become Honduras was made by Columbus on his third voyage. There he found Indians wearing gold ornaments; thus, from the beginning Honduras has been associated with gold.

Twenty years later, having heard of fabulous mines in the interior from which the Mayans extracted gold to build their temples, the infamous Cortez dispatched reconnaissance parties, the first of these under the leadership of Captain Gabriel Rojas. The discovery of working gold mines was recorded by Francisco Herrera in 1524 when he referred to a "a spacious plain called Olancho, ill-seated near to River Guayape, whence much gold has been taken."

In his first writings, Bernal Diaz, the famous historian and soldier who served under Cortez, mentioned that his leader's name was already "feared and respected even among the distant tribes of Olancho, where subsequently so many lucrative mines were discovered."

The next year Cortez and Diaz reached the river Guayape themselves. "We had already fought our way through hostile tribes to Olancho, which at present is called Guayape abounding in lucrative gold mines."

These and a score of other references convinced me of the historical basis for such a story. I had next to locate San Jorge de Olancho on an ancient map. It proved simple enough. The luckless town had been at the foot of Mt. Boqueron along a tributary of the Guayape River.

It remained to locate references to a natural disaster that buried the town. A publication by the Peabody Museum provided the first proof: "San Jorge was one of the early Spanish settlements in the valley and was destroyed by flood, resulting from an earthquake which broke a mountain barrier of a river in the adjacent hills forming a pass called El Boqueron."

As for the story of the Golden Madonna, I had as yet heard only fragments. It was on the eve of my departure for Mt. Boqueron that I discovered a book by William Wells published in the middle of the nineteeth century that gives a complete account of the story, including a warning to those who would venture there.

Honduras is a land of steep and continuous hills from which its name is derived. From the top of one of those hills, the view is reminiscent of a vast, brown and angry sea. Just three decades past, the road I was on, then the only one in the country, was nothing more than a ragged trail extending from Teguciagalpa towards San Pedro Sula on the Caribbean coast. It was known as The Road, and most who ventured upon it rode horses or walked. The well-to-do hired conveyances known as baronesses. These consisted of the stripped down chasses of American cars with homemade cabs slapped on top. The engine was wrapped in swaths of tire and the intake manifold stuck five feet straight up in the air, above the dust and protected from flooding rivers. These jerry-rigged charabancs were named to honour a fat and evil baroness who murdered her skinny and nearly as evil husband. A typically Honduran kind of hero.

Thievery is a national pastime and the roads are the special workplaces of the ladrones. But in a country where everybody is armed it is difficult to pick out the hold-up men. You never know until you're looking down a gun barrel. Twice on the trip to Mt. Boqueron, I came upon clusters of people stopping traffic with ropes stretched across the road, revolvers dangling from their hands, shotguns over their shoulders.

As I came to a halt, two masked figures wearing animal skins around their shoulders and dirty bedspreads that hung down below their knees emerged from the crowd. They held rusty paint cans.

144

Their masks were of hammered tin and fringed with hemp.

After I tossed some coins into the cans, the ropes were dropped, the crowd backed away and I drove off. In the rearview mirror, I saw them staring blankly after me.

Reaching Juticalpa, the nearest town to my destination, I figured I might venture in and obtain pertinent information, or at least some local lore. But if I believed in portents, I would admit one appeared to me on the edge of town: two grim-faced little girls assiduously throwing stones at an eight-foot-long crushed snake that lay across the road, its entrails spilled out into the dirt.

The dusty, rock-strewn road into town turned into a dusty, rock-strewn main street ending at a hard dirt plaza sadly sporting four gray and diseased palm trees. A church and a Shell station faced each other across a woebegone zocolo where even old men wouldn't come to sit. Out front of a line of shops were three people in wheelchairs; barely visible on the canvas backs of their chairs were the stenciled letters: Riverside Hospital.

I was the only customer in the only comedor open for business. The sullen proprietress took her time serving me coffee. Meanwhile I watched two little boys scooting around the floor flicking at pop bottle caps. An errant cap rousted a rat from behind a tin bucket in a corner, the scabrous rodent streaking across the floor and into a hole at the bottom of the opposite wall. Simultaneously, a bottle cap landed at my feet. I looked at the little boy who had sent it to me as a gesture of shy friendship. Bending down, with my index finger I propelled the cap over the dirty floor and through the rat's portal. The kid in the striped t-shirt went after it on his hands and knees and when he reached out towards the hole, I called, "No!"

He stopped, looked at me and at his mother who remained expressionless. Then he plunged his hand through the hole as she watched, waiting.

I took my coffee outside. Two soldiers in camouflage uniforms, carrying delicate-looking Israeli machine guns, unfastened themselves from a pole in front of the telephone office and came over, boots clacking on the board sidewalk. They stood and stared at me. I smiled; they stared. I finished my coffee and went over to the post office.

After receiving nothing but hostile stares for my inquiries from the woman and two men employees who were busy drinking, of all things, a bottle of champagne, I picked another road out of town for a little variety and to avoid the snake decomposing in the noonday sun.

Beyond Juticalpa, the road emerged into rangeland that would continue all the way to the Nicaraguan border. I scanned the mountains to the north, looking for Boqueron whose contours I knew perfectly from 150-year-old lithographs. Yet, despite my attentions, the first appearance of the mountains was a shock; it was as if the two adjacent mountains moved aside to reveal Boqueron in my peripheral vision.

I had thought of this place for a long time, had envisioned it, and now I felt that rare surge of excitement and expectation that is the heart of what is called adventure.

I followed the cattle trail on foot as far as it went, across the fields to the edge of the forest. I could hear the stream rushing somewhere through the trees. As I was lacing up my boots, a gaggle of boys appeared from the forest. Seven or eight of them, none more that 14-years-old. They approached shyly and their ringleader started asking questions. We shot the breeze for a few minutes before they got around to my purpose for being there. I told them I wanted to see Mt. Boqueron up close because it was a dormant volcano.

The boss kid, Olivero, volunteered to take me as far as a shack, a mile deep into the woods, that was the property of one of his uncles. I went with him after sending the other kids back to guard the jeep. Olivero was related to all the people around there, his entire extended family worked on the cattle ranches, always had and probably always would. I asked if he encountered many other foreigners wanting to see Boqueron. No, he replied, he hadn't seen a white person for two and a half years when three Germans, a woman and two men, had come to Boqueron.

"Oh, and what did they want?"

"To climb the volcano, senor."

"Me too, that's what I want to do. I'll come back another day with my equipment but today I just want to see the mountain up close."

As Olivero was giving me directions to the shack, a man emerged into the clearing from another path. Olivero waved him over. "You are fortunate, senor. This man is going past the spot where you might wish to start your climb."

Geraldo was short, stocky, with thick wrists and arms. He wore jeans, a blue t-shirt and a straw hat. In a leather sheath at his side hung the ubiquitous machete, tool of all work. Geraldo said the trail he followed to his village indeed passed a good spot to begin a climb of the mountain.

We set off and after a few minutes Geraldo asked me where my companions were. I told him that I had come alone. Soon the forest had become a jungle and before we plunged into the dark, I had him pose for a photograph.

We passed through a bower formed by wild orchids hanging from trees whose tops were lost in the unseen sky, and Geraldo turned to me again, "It is true, you are alone?"

"Yes, I'm alone," I said and we marched deeper into the jungle. It was a high afternoon but dark; no light peeked through the riotous tangle of vines and dripping leaves that made a tunnel around the rough trail and would claim it back quicker than a tryst with a Comayagu whore, were it not for peasants and their machetes.

The humidity seemed to get inside you and press outwards. I would have liked to stop and rest, if only to lean one hand against a tree and catch my breath, but no; I trudged along, adrenaline and exhaustion waging war in my body to match the struggle between jungle and machete. I kept going because I realized I had no choice. There was the broad back of Geraldo. The furrows in his brown neck. I realized I had no choice because Geraldo was going to try and kill me.

This became clear to me as we teetered along a narrow tree that had fallen over this tributary of the Guayape River, the water madly boiling thirty feet below. When I managed to get across, he looked at me with dismay. I knew.

Every now and then, he'd glance back over his shoulder, brows knitted, eyes like little pieces of broken glass. He was trying to put me in a position where I would be lost, exhausted, disoriented and at his mercy. I knew what he was thinking when he glanced at me. He was thinking: he hasn't tired yet, this gringo. He keeps going, on and on.

It wasn't going to be as easy as he thought.

The next time we stopped I was ready for it but it didn't come. The tip of his blade hung down around his boot top. He said we should pause for a moment to rest. As far as he knew, I was looking for the best place to start a climb of the mountain. I had said nothing about looking for gold. But now I asked him if once, long ago there had not been a town near here. He said that there had been.

"It was called Olancho-something?"

"Yes. Olancho Viejo. Or San Jorge."

"Buried by an avalanche is what I heard."

"Yes."

"What did the people do there?"

"I do not know; it was many centuries ago."

"Is it close to here?"

"Yes, it is not far."

We continued on, the trail getting steeper as it hugged the side of the mountain. I kept far enough behind so that if Geraldo suddenly pivoted and swung the blade at me instead of the flora, I would be beyond the arc but close enough to then step inside it.

Before us the river seemed to explode around a bend and crash against boulders that sat tall in the water like Easter Island statues.

This very moment, I knew, back in Tegucigalpa, the guy from the CIA was sitting poolside at the Honduran Mayan Holiday Inn discussing strategy with the Army officers. At a nearby table contemporary-style blow-dried missionaries from Atlanta, Georgia were deep in their concordances. Not too many kilometers to the east of where I was now, American troops were escorting Contras over into Nicaragua. My wife was waiting for me in a pretty town in Guatemala, and back in Vancouver—did it really exist?—they were just getting off work and heading for the beach. Meanwhile I was lost inside a legend and deep in the jungle.

We seemed to come around a side of the mountain, out of the darkness and into a sort of crepuscular light. The trail gradually descended to follow the river's edge, and Geraldo stopped for a drink. He put the machete away, bent and scooped water into his hands. He took a drink and bid me to do the same. I shook my head.

While Geraldo unctuously extolled the virtues of the, to me, poisonous water, I looked away up at the mountain and saw where a part of it had once been torn away by avalanche. I interrupted his pitch with a question, "The old town, it was at the foot of the mountain, directly in the path of the avalanche, yes?"

"Yes, yes," he nodded impatiently. "Have a drink, senor. You need water."

Ahead of us the river fell away from the foot of the mountain and the land opened up. There was still thick underbrush but fewer trees. Following the gouge in the mountain left by the slide, I stood where the land formed a knoll that lead to the river. The bank here was higher than on the other side. Looking toward the mountain, in the thick tangle of foliage that carpeted the jungle floor and crept up the sides of trees, I saw what looked, incongruously, like grey stones. I realized they were the remains of buildings.

Geraldo had kept talking. I was aware that he sounded agitated but I wasn't listening. I had found the place I was looking for. I was standing on top of a billion dollars worth of gold.

"Geraldo, is this where the old town was?"

"Yes, yes. But forget that. Come with me, my friend; my village is nearby. We go around the mountain to the other side. There you will find beer and women."

"No, thank you," I replied. "I think I've gone far enough."

I wanted to be by myself now to poke around the ruins. I took some bills from my pocket and handed them to Geraldo, thanking him for helping me. At first he studied the bills like he didn't grasp the meaning of what he held in his hand, as if lempuras were foreign to him

Then he went from feigning perplexity to acting offended. He declared that he was a poor man and I a rich one, and should give him more. I shook my head; what I had given him was quite generous. He named a greater figure and I said he would get no more money from me. He needed money for new boots, he said. "See how poor mine are?"

I looked at his boots and was actually thinking that they were no worse than my own, probably better, when he went for the blade. His hand moved in a blur, but I was close enough to leap and grab his forearm before the machete was half way out of the scabbard. I took his arm in both my hands, but he would not release the machete. He began to hit at my side with his other hand. I yanked his wrist back towards me and pushed down hard on his elbow.

Kneeling with one knee in the middle of his back, I kept him there on the ground by the river, his arm twisted up behind him. When he stopped struggling, and I had caught my breath, I lifted my knee and, while holding his arm, let him up.

He was still for a moment then jerked back with his free arm, trying to strike me with his elbow. I grabbed his ear, gave it a sudden, hard twist and he went down yelling like an angry baby and with no pride at all. I kept twisting and squeezing his ear—I could feel it getting hot—until he flung his free arm straight out in the dirt and his body went limp. Only then did I take the machete from him and move a few feet away.

The wooden handle was smooth and filled my hand. The machete was heavier than I would have thought. He looked up at me from all fours. I didn't want him to spring while I had the machete because I knew I wouldn't use it, and thus it would encumber me. I flung it out into the river and heard it clang against a rock.

I advised Geraldo to get up and get going. He took a few steps but looked over his shoulder to give me a parting sneer. I watched him disappear in the trees, one arm stiff and straight against his side.

It had all happened too fast for me to be scared or even angry. I felt strangely aloof, almost numb. Yet I knew I had to hurry on my way because his parting look did not bode well.

I started back the way we had come, in double time.

Geraldo would not hesitate to seek his revenge, I reasoned. I could have taken his head off with that machete; I could have tossed him in the river instead of the blade; I might have at least broken his arms and legs. Any of which he would have done to me if he had been smart enough or skilled enough. So, worse than merely foiling his plans was letting him up, the ultimate insult to his pride. And I had made him cry out. He had cried to a gringo; it must be like a worm turning in his gut.

I had not gone very far before I heard the call and answer of the whistles behind me. It sounded as if there were three different tones, one more frequent than the others. That must be Geraldo giving instructions to his pals. I had been crashing along trying to outdistance the noise, but I stopped to listen, to try and place them. The whistling ceased. It started again when I began to move. The whistling now sounded less fragmented. They were in concert and I knew damn well what the theme was.

The elemental nature of this did not escape me. It was a

prehistoric hunt in the forest primeval. In retrospect, I realize this was an experience almost exclusively beyond the context of modern, urban man. At the time, however, I wanted to run swiftly back into my own context.

After a few minutes it seemed as if the calls of one of the men were coming from the other side of the river and from behind me. I was nearly frantic when I realized their plan. Geraldo must have sent this guy over the river to block my crossing at the fallen tree. They wanted me right there, teetering thirty feet above the rocks and white water, and them waiting on either side.

I ran hard then, telling myself it would not happen; they would not catch me that way. And when I got there, I didn't even pause for a deep breath. I made the other side like Nijinsky crossing the stage, and there was nobody waiting.

Climbing the hill, in order to keep the river and the trail in sight, I moved through the cover of trees. By the time I reached the edge of the jungle, the whistling had stopped. There was a mile or so of forest and then a barn that marked the beginning of the cattle grazing land. That last bit I took nice and easy, so to appear composed for the benefit of the kids who would be guarding the jeep.

After distributing coins, I drove several of them, all brothers, to their home, a place made of mud, rock and straw in the middle of the fertile rangeland. There were half a dozen adults and twice as many children hanging around inside and outside of this bleak shanty. They all lived there, the oldest boy told me. They all worked for the local ranchers, as had their parents, forever. The adults stared at me with no curiosity and less warmth.

Back on the hard road I drove like hell to get away from there. Drove like hell for 30 kilometers until I hit a Contra roadblock. Nicaraguan Contras supported by the United States conducting a roadblock in Honduras. The Contras, by the way, did not exist in Honduras at the time, officially. They got me out of the car and went through it, searching the engine compartment, peeking inside the air cleaner, under the wheel wells. There was a gum chewing American in crisp, jungle issue. He didn't like my Canadian passport one bit, no doubt equating it with a soft attitude toward communism that went back past draft dodger times. I didn't escape from there until I started throwing around a few names that stuck in my mind from the Honduras Mayan, chief among them being that of the CIA man.

I stopped for gas at a settlement called Guaimaca and gave a ride to a man with a sick baby. He was going to his home at Comayagua. At Tapalanga where the road divides, I decided to take him to Comayagua instead of spending the night at Tegucigalpa.

It was a mistake. All tin-roofed, plaster shacks squatting in the dust. At the ends of these streets, chief among them being Ten Lemp Alley, named after the going rate, ten lempuras, were buses from the nearby U.S. army base letting off and picking up soldiers in jeans and t-shirts with obscene haircuts.

They swaggered into and stumbled out of brothels that featured bars with watered down, overpriced drinks, and blaring robotized consumer rock that must have been fed from a centralized monster computer back in God's country, a couple of sofas with girls in cheap dresses, faded halter tops or bras that had never been washed. In one place there was a sign over the bar: "Where's the Beef?"

Outside everyone was on the hustle; every cripple, degenerate, and amputee too messed up to make it to Tegu for Holy Week. And among this lot were two missionaries passing out tracts on venereal disease. A black soldier took one of these missives, noticed the letters A.I.D. and S., and thrust it angrily back at the missionary, "Shee-it I ain't no faggot!"

And over everything was the ineffable odour of another kind of disease. It was the stink of flat out corruption, that virulent, unrelenting bugger that found a willing host in Honduras a long time ago and wasn't about to leave.

Back in Tegucigalpa the next day, Good Friday, I found the

central square crowded with all the beggars, cripples and thieves who had been able to make it, who were willing to trust their fates to Paradise rather than Ten Lemp Alley. Along with them were hundreds of regular devout Catholics and a couple of dozen American missionaries.

The bleeding plaster body of Jesus was being carried solemnly into the church of St. Michael. In Latin America, St. Michael is the special guardian of the sick and they were all here today, braced and trussed, on roller boards, sores running through filthy, unravelling bandages. Among them stood the corn fed American Protestants, cracking side of the mouth jokes about papists while others of their number distributed pamphlets concerning "La Gran Pregunta."

Across the square from the church and at the foot of the statue of General Morazon, stood an elder of the Charismatic Church, U.S.A., singing Christian contemporary tunes in Spanish. The old general looming on his plinth had been the first to call for a United Central America and got killed for having the idea.

I checked into the Istmania Hotel on a narrow street off the marketplace. From the lobby one can look across to a sign in a window opposite that warns "Do not take Photographs of This Building."

Not so conspicuous, above the door, is the amalgram, Interpol. A vacant lot separates Interpol, the international police organization, from a three-storey export-import house run by Chinese. The lot is cut off from the street by a chain link, barbed wire topped fence. A teenager who looked like a thousand other Honduran street punks was pacing along the other side of the fence like a panther in a cage. He kept both hands around the butt of a .357 Magnum, barrel against his collar bone.

That night I stayed in my hotel room with my maps and notes spread before me. I thought about the two guys I knew in Canada, the gemologist and the geologist, who claimed to have been to the site of the buried city the year before. But their description of the place they had been to bore no resemblance to San Jorge. Also they said they had come upon the place by boat, which was impossible on the tributary of the Guayape I had followed. Furthermore, none of the people with whom I spoke had seen gringos for several years, those being three Germans, two men and a woman.

Soon I realized the mistake they had made.

When the avalanche destroyed San Jorge de Olancho, or Olancho Viejo, survivors fled across country and re-established themselves at a place they named Olanchito, or new Olancho. The modern Olanchito is a lively town on the navigable Aguan River. The local church displays the corona de cuerpo, the horsehide crown, supposedly taken from the head of the golden madonna. To add to the confusion there is a small settlement nearby called San Jorge de Olanchito.

The next day I spent on the street, wandering from the slums to the elegant quarter around the American embassy. I met a middle class Honduran couple, an engineer and his wife who worked for the United Nations and they provided me with a short course on the dull, relentless and official criminality that had robbed the spirit of an entire nation.

A mile past the embassy is an abandoned compound that once housed San Felipe hospital. Weeds grow between the old buildings, heavy chains are draped across heavy metal doors, windows are long gone; yet out front of one small, decaying stucco building, wash was hanging on a line and in the long grass in a wheelchair sat a gaunt woman with braces on her legs, her head lolling back and to one side and she smiled broadly and grotesquely. It was the first smile I had seen in all of Honduras.

In the late afternoon, I flagged down a cab on Embassy Row and asked the driver to take me to the Contra headquarters.

It was a six lemp ride to a beautifully maintained villa near the airport. A guard told me that the place was closed until Tuesday because of Holy Week. I asked him if he was sure this was the headquarters in Honduras of the Nicaraguan Contras. Certainly, he said, and if I wished to come back on Tuesday I would surely find people who would tell me whatever I wished to know.

Sunday, Americans and rich Hondurans sat around the pool of the Mayan in a drizzle. I read three day old newspapers.

That night while lying on my bed with a book, back at the Istmania, I received six Easter visitors. I heard a key in the lock of the door and before I could get up, in walked a man in a suit and five other guys with guns. I recognized two of them from the Interpol office, one was the punk with the Magnum. They grabbed me off the bed and, in the universal language of the rifle barrel in the belly, made it known that they wanted me against the wall.

At first, I feared this was somehow connected with San Jorge, and a charge of attempting to steal national artifacts. But no; I had been seen taking pictures all around town, and they wanted my film. They ripped the roll out of my camera, found two more and asked if I was a spy. I told them no; I was not a spy, no way.

They said I would have to pay them $100 U.S., or 200 lempuras to get my camera back. I replied that they could have the damned camera, upon which the boss nodded to one of his boys, who nodded back and chopped me in the ribs with the butt of his rifle. We negotiated. I wound up giving them $50 for the camera. After a parting shot to the belly, they left with the second smiles I had seen in all of Honduras.

But there was one roll of film unaccounted for, and I found it behind the skirt of the yellow ochre bedspread.

I had to catch a 6:30 flight the next morning for San Salvador and was at the airport before the doors opened. Waiting on the curb outside was the airport official I had wondered about when I arrived, the man whose face had been gone over with a straight razor. But only the right side of it; the left was unmarked like a vertical line had been drawn from his hair line to the tip of his chin.

He sat there for a few minutes picking his teeth and staring at me. Then he got up, spat out the toothpick and went around the side of the building.

I would like to say that as the Taca Airlines plane took off and I looked down at that airport that resembled a shack you find in the middle of an auto parts yard or nuclear waste dump in New Jersey, that I thanked my lucky stars for surviving and vowed never to return. But that would only be half true, and only a billion dollars, or some part of it, could make me go back to Honduras.

An hour later I was sitting in a cafe in San Salvador with a man whose first name was Jorge and whose last name was one of those of German origin so frequent in parts of Central and South America. It matters not about his position. Suffice to say all that was required for me to get through customs was a whispered word by him to the official in charge.

Jorge was discussing the saintly attributes of the local priest who at the moment was crossing the avenue in front of us. I took the opportunity to comment that while neither of my own patrons, the Greater and Lesser James' were particularly interesting members of the canon, his, Jorge, was at least a patron of soldiers and boy scouts.

"And, of course, he slew the dragon."

Jorge, Jorge de Olancho, St. George. I had been thinking of St. George and wondering why the Spaniards, coming upon the Indian town with its golden implements, its jewellery and storehouse of the precious, glittering metal, had named it after him.

I knew the curious thing about St. George was that, unlike with other saints, religious scholars endeavored to disprove the stories about him. One romancier after another, however, had gotten into the act, attributing to St. George all manner of wondrous deeds. The most fabulous of these stories, the one about him rescuing a maiden by slaying a dragon, was not devised until the late middle ages.

Perhaps it is entirely irrelevant but I have wondered many times whether the priests who named the town were aware that the story of St. George and the dragon was first published in a book called *The Golden Legend.*

WEEKEND IN SOWETO

I t is early on a Saturday morning in 1978. The end of June and the beginning of winter. The earth is bare but for the tall elephant grass, brown and so brittle now that it rasps like women's stockings as we make our way down the hill from Orlando East. I am thankful for even the weak sunlight filtering through the dishwater sky, for I have just woken from a cold and fitful sleep on the dirt floor of a cardboard-walled addition to the two-room house in which Simon's mother and his six brothers and sisters sleep. Simon walks ahead of me, chanting a song in Sotho, his own language. His singing and the elephant grass impress upon me: Africa. The vast sweep of regimented rooftops below and the searchlights mounted ominously on their towers impress upon me: Soweto.

Soweto is an acronym formed from the first two letters of the words South Western Townships; it rhymes with ghetto. The area originally consisted of makeshift homes—known as locations—for black workers who were not permitted to live (and still aren't) in Johannesburg. When the National Party came to power in 1948 it bulldozed the locations in the name of slum clearance and built new, cheap housing.

Hardly anyone outside of Africa knew Soweto existed until

June, 1976, when the ghetto erupted in an orgy of riot and murder. "Rampaging black youths" battled armed police and occupied the TV screens of the world. During an official daytime tour, my government guide blamed the outbreak on hoodlums, agitated by outsiders. "They burned their own buildings and killed innocent people. The leftwing press said it was a protest by children. Yes. Children in their 30s."

Simon, my guide for a very unofficial tour of Soweto that night, explained things differently: "It started as a peaceful march by students to the Bantu education offices in Johannesburg. They were protesting the use of Afrikaans, a language that has been forced upon us. The police ordered us to disperse. When we didn't they opened fire." At least 700 blacks died in the fighting.

It had not been easy to get into Soweto, even in the afternoon, particularly during the anniversary of the riots. You need a government permit, which is available only for purposes of official business or Escorted Visits by Interested Parties. The latter is the same tour given to journalists and consists of three hours of government propaganda. The official line is that foreign journalists arrive with preconceptions that obscure the realities. The basic "reality" is that the government is altruistically lifting the blacks out of the Stone Age. A "typical misconception" is that South Africa is a slough of racism. My guide, a 38 year old woman of Greek and English descent who immigrated to South Africa 10 years ago, believes it to be "the greatest country in the world." Despite what journalists see here she says, they still write puerile stories.

But to enter as a journalist you must be approved by the government. And a government that does not allow anyone of a supposed radical nature to talk with more than one person at a time is hardly going to allow suspect journalists into the country, much less into Soweto.

On my entry card I put down "teacher," hoping they would not ask me of what, and stated my reason for wishing to visit Soweto as tourism. It was the right thing to say. My government guide greeted me with a smile and an enthusiasm that allowed me to see myself through her eyes: a malleable mind. I wanted her to talk freely and she did.

Our Volkswagen tour bus was driven by a young black named David. He remained solemn-faced while she released a litany of figures to show how much the whites had done for their burden, the blacks. So many homes, so many schools, so many swimming pools. "See, now we are in Soweto and you probably didn't even realize it, did you? You expected maybe barricades and barbed wire, eh? Well, look at the houses, how nice they are. And this is not the best section of Soweto by any means. It is a typical one. Here is a map. You can follow our route and you'll see that I'm showing you all of Soweto and not just special places to impress foreign visitors."

Yes, parts of Soweto look tidy. In fact, it is disconcerting to see that the houses built for blacks are far superior to those built for Indians on Canadian reserves. Compared to black ghettos in the United States, Soweto is Don Mills. But for the bare earth, the junk-strewn yards, the light towers and the blank, black faces, we could be in a working class subdivision anywhere. It is a matter of great pride to the government official, a justification of her government. But there is a troubling inconsistency. The government has built more than 100,000 houses for a legal population of 858,334 (the real figure is closer to 1.5 million). Even using the official figures, that is 8.5 people per two-room house.

My guide related how each house originally had a fruit tree in the front yard. "In hopes that these people would take some pride in their surroundings. You don't see any fruit trees around do you?"

"No," I said. But I recalled another government statistic: 18,000 homes have electricity. One in nine. There had been snow flurries earlier that morning and it was still cold. I wondered whether the fruit trees hadn't long ago been converted to fuel.

"We had hoped they would plant gardens too, but they don't seem to have any pride."

David didn't even flinch.

Of course in South Africa, white nationalists feel themselves innately superior to the black man. In North America only the most blatant racist would publicly admit to this attitude, but in South Africa it underlines all government procedure. My guide considered herself a liberal. I was reminded of that late—'60s definition of a liberal: someone two steps to the left on any issue until it affects him personally, at which time he assumes his natural position—two steps to the right. This lady had taken two steps to the right and kept going. A Joberg liberal, she believed her government had done much for the blacks. She believed blacks were better off in South Africa than anywhere else in the world. "The real problem here," she said, "is that blacks will do nothing to help themselves." To her, the idea that blacks be allowed to vote in their native country is not so much untenable as it is ludicrous. Even black leaders don't want universal suffrage, she assured me. One such man is Credo Mutwa, a witchdoctor and writer. "He had to hide during the riots. They tried to kill him because he wouldn't join in."

Later, I was shown the house of Richard Maponya, a businessman and politician. "He's a millionaire. He drives a Mercedes Benz. He's an example to his race."

That evening I was sitting at a table in Chirwelco with Simon, drinking a tall glass of cane spirit. We were in a shebeen, a dive where anything can happen—and often does. A few days earlier a Johannesburg newspaper had referred to shebeens as "cesspools and fertile breeding grounds for crime."

It was my first drink of the evening and I hoped it would calm me down. I had received several cold-chisel stares when I came in; only Simon's eloquence saved me. "It cool, man. It cool," he urged. After that they seemed to accept me.

Half an hour earlier I had made my second entrance into Soweto, this time hiding in a pile of laundry in the back of Simon's station wagon. Simon is a friend of a friend of a contact on one of the

Johannesburg newspapers. Had we been caught, he probably stood to get in more trouble than me. I was not quite sure why he took the risk.

"Ever since '76," Simon said over our drinks, "Soweto has been quiet. In comparison to the way it used to be. Before, man, all the time jumping. The cats and chicks, they did their thing all night. Soon as school and work was over it start to jump. . . . Drink up and we will try to find some action."

Simon wanted to show me the extremes of the social spectrum and we started at the bottom—a beer hall where middle-aged men sat at wooden tables hoisting quart bottles under bare light bulbs. It reminded me of pubs in Canada where men, mostly immigrants, drink themselves into oblivion to forget their pasts. Here, they were drinking True Beer, a stupefying concoction brewed from sorghum that tastes like a mixture of yogurt and Guinness Stout. I tried to reconcile this morose scene—100 men in cheap, ill-fitting western clothing—with all those naive, antiquated notions of Africa.

Outside, a gang of teenagers was kicking at a middle-aged man who lay on the ground. Two youths rifled his pockets while several others stood over him with their weapons, sharpened bicycle spokes. As we drove away, Simon told me these gangs of unemployed Zulu teenagers, called Tsotsis, terrorize the residents.

I always considered Zulus more aggressive and warlike than other tribes. Simon explained, "Yes, but that has not always been true. Zulus were farmers and shepherds for thousands of years until the time of Shaka and Dingane. These were bad chieftains like Stalin. Like Hitler. Many Zulus fled to work for white men and some were captured and taken to America as slaves. They were the lucky ones. These Tsotsis are the descendants of those who did not flee. The hooligans of Soweto who kill their own kind."

After a moment, he added: "There are better things to do with their violent tendencies."

"Yes?"

He chewed his lip as he hesitated. "Look there are 70,000 of us gone north to training camps. Mozambique, Angola. We'll begin to return soon."

We edged through Pimville, where the searchlights carved harsh paths through the streets, ferreting out doorways, automobiles and people. Everything looked sinister. We pulled up before a place called the Diepkloof Hotel along the main road to Johannesburg. "This is where the other half meets. The situations hang out here. It is owned by The Man, Mr. WRAB.

"Situations" is a term used in the townships to denote people of high social standing, such as the doctors from Baragwaath Hospital (for non-Europeans) across the road from the hotel. Mr. WRAB, The Man or Mr. Jones, is otherwise known as the West Rand Administration Board.

Inside, the lounge was all plush carpeting, dim lights and smooth conversation. A recording of Dorothy Moore filtered through the speakers, low and silky. It was the kind of place where examples to their race came to sip wine and taste cheese. No Tsotsis in here.

The refined atmosphere in the hotel was in stark contrast to the mayhem across the street. Vehicles arrived at the emergency entrance like ambulances in a speeded up movie, carrying victims of the weekend carnage. Up to 20 reported murders each Friday and Saturday night. Fifty reported criminal homicides. A weekend in Soweto. I wondered which car bore the body of the man the Tsotsis had worked over.

The Baragwanath Hospital is a prime topic for government spokesmen. An excellent example of what South Africa is doing for its blacks, it also allows a sharp dig at the propensity for crime and indiscriminate pregnancy. Including assaults, stabbings, bullet wounds and other assorted beatings, Bara treats 1.1 million outpatients and 85,000 ward cases a year, making it the busiest hospital in the country. As for population growth, it is higher among blacks in South Africa than it is in India. There are 70 births a day at

163

Baragwanath. I was glad when Simon suggested the next stop on the agenda.

"Now we go to do some swinging."

We went to a place called the Pelican in Orlando East. The people seemed to exist in a kind of sartorial time warp. Men in pleated trousers and loose shirts were swinging women in toreador pants or flouncy skirts and clunky wedge-heeled pumps; it was all reminiscent of some late 1940s jitterbug contest. Dark faces glistened with sweat. The shouting, the sense of celebration were typical of Friday nights everywhere, but here there was more energy, as though taking one's mind off all the rest of it, the world outside the nightclub, required extraordinary exertion. The music ranged from country and western to the Philadelphia sound of Harold Melvin to hard bop. Everyone kept dancing and drinking, paying special attention to the strange white man on the floor. There was no hostility—for now.

I slept fitfully and the morning was cold. We made our way down the hill through the elephant grass toward the car; Simon had parked it in back of the soccer stadium. Sheltered by the overhang of the bleachers, an old man in a tattered greatcoat unfolded a wooden board and set it in the dust. From a huge pocket he took a tin can, placed it beside the board and then squatted on his haunches, his back against the wall. Simon told me he was an old con man who made his living at Koopie dice. He told me to address him as Old Gentleman.

The man nodded to me. I squatted down beside him. He had a glass eye; white whiskers bristled his chin. His board was a parallelogram divided into squares. I put a 20-cent piece down. He shook the dice out of the can onto the board, grunted and picked up my coin.

"So you have come to see the townships," he said as I put down another 20-cent piece.

I told him where we had been. He shook a long, cracked,

brown finger at Simon. "If I was your age I would spend no time in spots."

"What would you be doing, Old Gentleman?" I asked.

He looked at me and then at Simon and back to me. He grinned wickedly. "When I was a young one I came to Joburg to work in the gold mines and break my back. Every time I bent over the white man got richer and I got nothing. Yeah."

He arched an eyebrow at me for another play.

"I thought, that the way it is. Way it has to be. That was then. They put us here and we know nothing. Now I know but it too late. For me. Not for you." He wagged his finger once again at Simon.

Then he fixed his eye on me and waved the dice can in the air, indicating all of Soweto. "It time has come."

The dusty streets were filling up now. People were leaving their houses and congregating at the bus stops, filing toward the trains, jumping into taxis. They were going to Johannesburg to spend their pay cheques, or to window-shop, or to listen to the exhortations of Witchdoctor Sam, who held court in Diagonal Street. Bleak streets were thronged with people. A million and a half people in Soweto. Four blacks in South Africa for every white.

In a shebeen at night Soweto had seemed timeless, permanent, but in the morning it felt tenuous, as though its boundaries were arbitrary and could never contain its people. Its time was coming, certainly.

Staying Alive In Bogota

A rturo Amundez is worried. He sits in the chrome and mirror bar of the Hotel Tequendania in Bogota rubbing his chin and thinking. It is 1979. He is about 30 years old and affluent and he knows that by rights he should be neither. He never knew his mother, and his father is a handful of tenuous memories Amundez is no longer sure he didn't invent. He grew up on the squalid, mean streets of this Bogota. He lived in them, slept in them, begged in them and worse. From the time he was 4 until he was 13, Amundez doubts that he slept in a bed more than 10 times. He was one of the gaminos, street urchins who exist by eating garbage or sneaking into restaurants to stare pathetically at your plate of food like wounded puppies in velvet paintings.

The most Amundez should have hoped for was to be a waiter or a newspaper vendor. He should never have been a successful businessman sitting in the most expensive hotel in Bogota, staring through tinted windows at the park where Sunday lovers are strolling and vagabonds are sleeping. One of the latter is now opening his bedroll, a tattered blanket wrapped around several newspapers, his hair is matted, his feet visible through the soles of his shoes. But Amundez is not thinking: "There but for the grace of God...." No, he is too worried for that. It's business that's got him down. There are new people entering the field and they are trying to force him out.

Amundez is in the cocaine business. He has enough paste in the lab to produce three kilograms of the stuff. When it is ready he can get it out for small change, and if he has a customer it will sell for $9,000. He had a deal lined up when he put the paste in the lab, but *they* moved in on him, and *they* are liable to move in on the next one too, because *they* are taking over. *They* are organized crime. Amundez says the real Corsican thing. Not the *mafiosa criolla*, the home-grown imitation. This is the legitimate article.

Amundez swings around on his stool and stares at his face in the mirror by the bar. It is a fine featured face, almost delicate in the muted blue light. His nose is thin, his chin fragile and cleft. You wonder how he has survived in a town where human life does not have much currency. It is almost an aristocrat's face, but for its brownness. There were surely a few grandees, a few *conquistadors*, mixed in with the Indians. His hands are dark and small like a parrot's claws. He has dark brown hair waving back from a high forehead. Well-tailored chocolate brown suit, a knit sport shirt, woven brown leather loafers. He is dressed like the pimp he once was.

He has survived because he is oh so cool, very smart and well armed. But he is an independent operator in a country where eventually an independent operator meets, not his match, but forces beyond his control.

The current Columbian Government calls itself a democracy, but a very few people control the lives of 25 million others. Forget about coffee and emeralds: the big business here is cocaine. It would take someone's sweet grandmother not to realize that a government that has a piece of everything has a piece of the biggest pie. There were not exactly barricades awaiting the Corsicans when they marched down to Bogota, which after all began as the camp for bandits looking for Eldorado.

We order a couple more *aguardentes*, a Pernod-type drink,

which come in delicate glasses with stems. Arturo Amundez is reminiscing in English good enough that it need not be rendered here in Mexican bandito dialect. He also gets by in Portuguese, French and German. You can't hustle a tourist unless you speak the language. "I never have known where I come from," he says. "One day I am just in existence in Bogota. I think I remember being in a *residencia* with some people who must have been relatives. Maybe I dream it. I have been always a child on the streets. I don't even know who I am really."

"What do you mean?"

"I am the man with no name. As a boy we banded together, us *gaminos*. One who was older, maybe 8 or 9, would pick two companions younger than himself. He would lead us to a restaurant or *pasteleria* and push us in the door to silently beg. The first time I did this the older boy gave me the name Arturo. Amundez was the name of a gangster in a Mexican cinema. He is a tough *caballero*."

We finish the drinks and leave the Tequendania. The cab drivers are lined up at the curb waiting to take advantage of tourists. We head down Carerra 7 toward La Candelaria, the ancient section of the city, soon passing La Esmeralda, a movie theatre whose marquee announces *Las Mujeres Saben del Amor*, the women who know all about love.

"When I was still a boy I became a pimp." Amundez says. "It was the first money I ever had I didn't steal. I was a pickpocket. There were little girls on the street also with no homes. I would take them to the schools of the rich kids and sell them. But it was not much money. Later big girls made me money. I did everything. Stole traveller's cheques and sold them. When the hippies started coming here from North America I began to get wealthy. They are so rich and stupid. They have lived soft lives and are easily parted from their money. They would come hollering "Coca! Coca! and I sold it to them. Then I'd go and help them out of jail when they got caught at the airport. So they pay me twice.

"Whenever I had money as a kid I went to see American

gangster movies. If I had enough money to eat or see a movie I went to the movie. I like Lee Marvin. My other hero in the world is Carlos Monzon, the Argentine. You know of him?"

"Probably the best fighter in the world."

Amundez nods, looks at me differently. "I believe in *machismo*. In being a man. That is important to me. It has kept me alive. Monzon is what it means to have *machismo*. Now come with me."

We turn the corner. Across the street there is an old brown horse with splayed hoofs standing patiently while a flatbed wagon is loaded with rotting fruit and vegetables by a short man in a suit and hat. His three kids are with him. They are brothers and they have a big dog with curled and matted hair the color of burnt sienna. Amundez stops to talk to a man in a red-and-white 1957 Mercury. The man starts to reach into his pocket, then looks at me and back at Amundez, who tells him it's all right. The man finishes the gesture, handing over a thick roll of peso notes. Amundez introduces me. The man is called Didi.

Amundez leads us into a *pasterleria*, a bakery, and we go into the back. The *pasterleria* is operated by Didi's brother. It serves as Amundez's operations centre. It is dark and the floor is wet. Amundez opens a door and we are in a tiled patio. A roof of sorts had been fashioned from scrap wood and tin. Light comes through the cracks. Amundez opens a shed and takes out a plastic bag filled with marijuana and two little painted tin boxes. He lifts the lid of one and I see the crystalline white powder. He puts the bag down and brings a knife out of his pocket. The blade jumps out. He dips the tip into the powder and holds it perfectly still under my nose. I snort and my nostrils buzz and go dry.

"It don't do nothing for me." Amundez says. He opens the other box, which contains a brown paste. "I'm going to roll *pistoleros*." He takes a scale out of the shed. "And I fix a few ounces to sell. Then I hit the streets. Check out the Hilton. I got to get my stuff from the lab."

"Okay," I say. "I'll see you around."

"Keep the faith."

Never is he so unhip as to refer to it as cocaine. He talks about nose candy or snow. He has a good job: T.V. producer, male model, real estate dealer. He has to have a good job to be able to afford the white powder that he places in a tiny spoon dangling against his chest. Not to mention the fresh $100 bill he likes to roll tight to transfer the line of cocaine up into his nostrils. He is a walking advertisement for the perfect drug of the 1970's: a highly hyped powder that's expensive and doesn't do much, a fact he happily overlooks because the stuff is, you know, heavy. Dynamite.

This dude is the end of a chain that begins with the Indian farmers who grow coca leaves high in the mountains of Columbia and Bolivia. They take special care cutting the plants back to get three or four harvests of plump leaves a year. When mature the leaves are processed in wooden crates or oil barrels. They are soaked in kerosene, then the liquid is drained off and the leaves discarded. The brown residue clinging to the sides and bottom of the crates is the paste that Amundez was going to mix with marijuana or tobacco and roll in cigarettes to give to Didi to sell around town. These are called *mixtos* or *pistoleros*.

The next step is the chemist. The paste is treated very carefully with hydrochloric acid. The result is the famous white powder. A trafficker can buy from the farmer and employ the chemist, or buy from the chemist himself. Bogota is filled with restaurants and *pastelerias* and blank doorways beyond which the white powder is produced. One kilogram can be purchased in Bogota for $3000. A kilogram is not terribly difficult to get out of the country if you have obtained it from the proper sources. Bogota's nickel and dimers, will, however, sell you the cocaine and then report you to Customs. When you are caught you have to bribe your way to freedom. The man you have bribed then splits the money with the man who sold you the cocaine. People try to take cocaine out in aerosol cans, false heels, false suitcase bottoms, in souvenirs. Any place and any way the human mind can think of. Most often it is crammed, rammed or shoved up the body's orifices.

Back home the enterprising smuggler divides his key into two keys, usually cutting it (stepping on it) with lecithin or lactose. Any smart cocaine dealer will try to get rid of his product in the biggest quantity possible. He knows that cocaine does not have a long shelf life. It is perishable. If he broke it down and dealt ounces he would make a higher profit, but there is the hassle of having to step on it again. Besides, the two keys will bring him $6,000.

The keys are usually bought by ounce dealers, and the first thing they do is step on it another time. The product is now 20 to 30 percent cocaine hydrochlorate, and there is still another link in the chain. Even an ounce of cocaine sells for $1500. So you have the gram dealer, and he too breaks out the lecithin. In fact if it gets you high down there at the gram level it probably isn't coke at all. The facsimile is sometimes more potent than the genuine article. Since most people who use cocaine know little about it, it's easy to cheat. A gram of coke is often lecithin or lactose combined with Novocain and amphetamine.

So our dude with the clipped mustache, coiffed hair, and coke spoon dangling on his chest is fortunate if the powder he snorts up his nostrils is even 10 percent cocaine. By the time it has traveled from the Andes to his dinner party he might be better off with a Tequila Sunrise.

I run into Didi on the street and he gives me a ride back to the *pasteleria*. Amundez is there and we go for a walk. "I want you to do me a favour if you will." he says. "It will be worth your while."

Amundez wants to use my room in the Hotel Regina for a deal that night. There is too much heat around his usual haunts. The Corsicans or somebody have been around. People are telling him that strange characters have been asking about him.

Amundez has an American who is going to buy all three keys. The American lives in a coastal town in Columbia where he's the only foreigner. Call him Harold Hockley and the town Bellavista. He works for a German-American company and is sick to death of Bellavista. He wants out, but he's having trouble with the Columbian government over his income tax. He needs more money, big money, to get out.

Since he runs the port and knows the crews on ships from all over the world, Hockley figures he is in a splendid position to get rich in the cocaine business. He is approached all the time by sailors wanting the white powder for which the country is so famous. Just last week a cook from one of the ships told him he had bought dozens of chickens in Bellavista and was frantically looking for cocaine to put inside them. He figures he would stuff the chickens and freeze them. Perfect. Hockley had used his two week vacation to come to Bogota and investigate.

Hockley is also after women. There are no whores in Bellavista, and the other women you have to marry. This is where Amundez comes in. "I size people up quickly. He knows nothing about cocaine and is scared. I see his weakness is for women and I work on that. I brought a beautiful young girl to him at the Hilton. It's one of the three hotels in Bogota where you can bring a girl. Also where we are going, the Bacata, where I have to sell some stuff."

Amundez does a lot of business in the Bacata. He has a perfect setup there. One of his former working girls now has a job behind the bar. He bought the job for her. "She keeps her ears open for me. She told me about Hockley."

Amundez shows up at my room about 7 toting a National Airlines flight bag from which he extracts a couple of shirts, two bakery boxes and a couple of *cafe tintos*. From one of the bakery boxes he takes a pound cake and from the other a plastic bag containing 6.6 pounds of snow white cocaine. He cuts the cake with his switchblade and we sit on the bed waiting for Hockley to arrive.

Soon there is a knock at the door. Amundez's face freezes. He checks his digital watch, 7:30. Hockley is not due until 8. Amundez reaches under his coat and brings out a .25 caliber Browning automatic. He hands it to me and then takes a clumsy old police special from the small of his back. "If that's not an American," he says "start firing."

There's another knock. We stand on either side of the door. I unlock it, step back and say "Come in."

The door opens and the man standing there turns a sudden, ghastly white. He backs away looking from one of us to the other. Amundez puts his gun away. I am relieved. Participatory journalism has its limits.

"I said 8 o'clock," Amundez says.

"Gee," Hockley exclaims in a southern accent. "I didn't have anything to do so I, well, I didn't think there was no harm in coming by early."

He is a short, dumpy, 40 year old man with a profile like a hawk and a hairline that encroaches on his forehead. Amundez asks if he wants a piece of cake. "Hell, no. What I need's a drink."

Amundez doesn't laugh. He shows Hockley the cocaine, takes a retractable scale from the flight bag and measures out the white powder. Hockley has never tried cocaine before. Amundez offers him some on the tip of his knife blade. Hockley's brown eyes go liquid as he sniffs and holds his nose. "Yes, yes," he says. "It's very nice."

We sit on the bed and Hockley opens his shirt to reveal a white stomach drooping over his money belt. He counts out hundreds on the bedspread—90 Ben Franklins. Amundez nods and Hockley picks up the bag of cocaine. He looks confused. Amundez smirks and hands him the flight bag.

When Hockley has left, Amundez says, "Come with me to eat Churasso and drink Chilean wine. I know the best place in Bogota."

I had to leave Bogota, but when I get back a month later I

look up Amundez again. He gets around with a cane now. He looks very weak and unhappy sitting by the shed in back of the *pasteleria*. He'd been shot in the leg when a couple of Corsicans, as he calls them, broke up a big deal he had put in motion. "It's finished here," he says. "The outsiders have taken over for good. I can do better taking a pound to Miami than dealing five keys here."

"How are you going to do that?"

He smiles faintly and takes out a Venezuelan passport. "I go up to Cartagena. I'm a rich Venezuelan on vacation. I go to Caracas and join the shopping brigade to Miami. Mira, the Mafia owns it all now. They're paying the government big money to own it all."

When I leave, Amundez escorts me out, limping to the door. I start to go when I remember the clipping in my pocket. It is part of an article from an old *Ring Magazine* about Carlos Monzon, the boxer. In the article Monzon tells what macho means. Monzon had been knocked down in one of his last fights but he had got up off the canvas to win it. Afterward his son came to the dressing room and told Monzon he'd cried when he was knocked down. Monzon told his son that getting up off the canvas was the real test. The real measure of a man, of *machismo*, was not in swaggering but in being hurt and coming back. I gave the clipping to Amundez.

Amundez reads it and puts it in his wallet. He gives me that faint smile and nod of the head. "See you in Miami," he says. "That is if I get out alive."

ON THE CADDY TRAIL

It was night. We had just crossed the state line from Tabasco into Chiapas, and the five men with guns stepped out of the bush and stopped the pickup truck. There were two of us inside. The driver was a Mexican in his thirties.

The bandits talked rapidly, moving in and out of the headlights, pointing the guns at us, shining flashlights in our eyes. Scarves covered the lower parts of their faces, and two of them wore berets. They were definitely not Chiapas campesinos, more like post-graduate students playing the part of revolutionaries. One guy pulled the scarf down off his face, stuck the barrel of the gun in my stomach and told me I should show more respect since he was Sub-Commandante Marcos. I actually was on the verge of quipping, "Yeah, and I'm Emiliano Zapata," but common sense overcame me.

The last time I'd had a weapon pulled on me in these parts was in 1987. That man, in Honduras, had been inspired by hunger and poverty, these punks were goaded by ideology and, thus, far more dangerous.

They beat my companion nearly senseless. I didn't learn why for several hours or until he was capable of speaking.

As he lay writhing and whimpering in the dirt, the bandits

demanded to know my story. I told them the truth and it felt peculiar as I listened to myself talk, accompanied by cricket sounds on the hot night air. Am I really telling them this? Are they taking it in?

Senores, I have not come to meddle in local affairs but am an artist tracing the 160 year old route of another artist, John Herbert Caddy, a Canadian like me, who was the first person to bring back reliable information about the legendary Mayan ceremonial centre of Palenque. Also like him, I travelled overland from Belize City and across the Peten region of Guatemala. And no one in Canada has ever heard of this guy, a special individual, I said.

One of them, not faux-Marcos, declared that is always the way. But faux-Marcos called me a liar because there is no road west from Flores, across four thousand square miles of the Peten. I replied that is exactly what one would believe if one relied on the maps. But there is, indeed, something that passes for a road and even something that passes for a bus and I had been on both. He divested himself of a shrug and a smirk and then they took my money—or at least the cache I was keeping in the event of robbery, about 74 dollars. When they seemed inclined to put me on the ground next to the driver because the amount wasn't very impressive, I offered up a CIBC bankcard that expired six years ago. The gun barrel again in my stomach produced a PIN number. A couple of minutes later, as they were about to disappear into the dark at the side of the road, Marcos, hoping to trip me up, asked for the PIN number again. I wasn't dumb enough to have made something up, no, I had given him my girl friend's year of birth.

I drove away and my companion huddled against the door, groaning through clenched teeth. As we approached his home town, he managed to explain that he had been beaten because his uncle ran for office with the wrong political party. At the home of his relatives, including the politician, I was fussed over and overfed.

Two days later I was at Palenque in the vault where Caddy inscribed his name in the ancient stone in 1840, and only then did the

Canadian artist seem real.

Oh, there had been a few Mayan explorers before him, no more than two or three, and those who purported to describe the ruins couldn't help but theorize about Atlantis or Lemurians, and sketch dinosaurs posing by the stelae. But Caddy never got any credit for what he accomplished. The reason why is a story in itself. Read through the extensive literature on the Maya, general or obscure, and you won't find his name. Look at the earliest pictures and none bear his signature. The credit for being the father of Mayan archaeology does not go to him but to John Lloyd Stephens. It is not Caddy but Frederick Catherwood, a less accomplished draftsman, who is the ubiquitous recorder of Central American antiquities.

Years ago in a store in Antiqua, Guatemala I found a tattered copy of a book called *Palenque: the Walker-Caddy Expedition to the Ancient Mayan city; 1839-1840.* It is edited by David M. Pendergast of the Royal Ontario Museum in Toronto who in the late-Sixties had learned of Caddy's unpublished journal and drawings and located them among the belongings of Caddy's great-granddaughter in Oakville, Ontario. I had never heard of Caddy or the expedition, nor had anyone else I questioned. What's more, the journals made for great reading. Not only did they describe an adventure filled with peril and excitement but they were what exploration literature never—ever—is: they were funny.

Well, Caddy was just the kind of person I've always been drawn to: a creative adventurer, an original who wouldn't buckle under. Similarly, it is Burton I like, not Speke or Stanley; not Thomas Edison but the French poet Charles Cros who really invented the phonograph; the master of the balloon and the first man to fly an airplane, the mercurial Alberto Santos-Dumont rather than the dullard Wright brothers.

Like them, Caddy never got his due. Had he been a careerist and played by the rules, the fellow would have made something of himself. And he probably would have left his laughter on the shores of

Belize City.

Which is where the whole thing started; where Caddy, from the Eastern Townships of Quebec, an engineer with the Royal Artillery, was stationed; where John Lloyd Stephens, accompanied by his close friend, Frederick Catherwood, alighted from the brig Mary Ann on October 31, 1939.

Stephens was a New Jersey-born lawyer with an interest in antiquities. In 1839, he used his contacts to secure an appointment as United States' Minister to Central America. Stephens never let official duties interfere with his explorations. In 1842, he published his two–volume Incidents of Travel in Central America, Chiapas and Yucatan. It is generally considered to be one of the great books of exploration literature, and it's never been out of print. But one thing it is not, is funny.

The first thing Stephens did in Belize City was present his credentials to the Superintendent of British Honduras, Colonel Alexander MacDonald. Stephens admitted his purpose had less to do with governing than with getting to Palenque, via a roundabout route that would include visits to other ruins. Macdonald, the sly old fox, regaled Stephens with war stories and, immediately, once the American was gone, began hatching his own scheme for getting to Palenque. There were fabulous rumours about the place but no reliable information. If the Americans got there first, MacDonald reasoned, Great Britain might somehow be put at a disadvantage.

Stephens and Catherwood set off the next day on a coastal steamer headed south. No sooner had MacDonald waved his last bye-bye than he got hold of a local official named Patrick Walker and told him he must get to Palenque before the Americans. Walker was a judge, president of the local regatta club and generally a civic busybody but he was no an explorer. He assembled a group of 29 other men with John Herbert Caddy, of the Royal Engineers, and an artist, as his second-in-command. When local newspapers became apprised of the two expeditions, they touted a "Race to Palenque."

When Stephens first saw Belize City from the water, he declared there was no sin in comparing it to such venerable old burgs as Venice and Alexandria. It looks pretty good in Caddy's sketches too. One hundred and sixty years later, gangs patrol the streets and urchins pass the time throwing rocks at bloated dog and rat corpses floating in the canals. Guidebooks are in agreement that there is no particular reason to visit Belize City but if such a thing becomes necessary one should not go out at night. The writers of those guidebooks probably never stayed in a Belize City hotel room.

Stephens left in a steamer, Caddy in a pitpan, a forty foot boat carved from a single tree, and me in a van with a born-again, cocoa-coloured Christian named Ned at the wheel. His work was to call at prisons and spread the word of Jesus.

Once he discovered I was a Canadian, Ned told me he feared the love of God was not strong enough to defeat the real culprit to his country—Americanism. They were coming down here, Americans, upsetting the economy and corrupting the people.

At first glance the town of San Ignacio is dusty, dirty and ugly, cars careening around corners scattering chickens and barefoot natives, and so hot that even the music from the CD store seems reluctant to spill out of twin speakers hanging over the broken sidewalks. At second glance, San Ignacio is much the same but you adjust the focus a bit and everything falls into place. There is a rhythm and a complex of social relations that makes it fascinating. The second glance shows the interplay of race—Mayan and black and white, and the myriad of mixtures—as well as language—Spanish and English—and all of it carries over into the music, food, and social life. But my second glance would come several weeks later. I had Caddy's route to follow.

I rode a packed, forty year old Blue Bird school bus (made in Atlanta, Ga.) west twenty miles through undulating ranchland with somebody's one year old daughter in my lap. She stared at me with big eyes the whole way. I never saw who put her there. When I was ready to get off, I handed her to the nearest person who presumably passed her along, like a hotdog at a ballgame, to where she belonged.

Shouldering my bag, I set off down a dirt road toward the Belize River and a hostelry that I had learned about from my friend Kevin Brown whom I was to meet in a few days at Tikal, the Mayan centre in Guatemala. The establishment consisted of an open air dining room and several bungalows along the river near a waterfall. It was run by a Mayan woman on land that is part of the family ranch. She told me that under the ground upon which I walked were ancient monuments of her people. I realized that the same could be said of the entire country.

I stayed at the falls for a few days to have a look at the country the way Caddy would have seen it, without modern distractions. One day, I walked back along the river in the direction of San Ignacio and crossed a swinging bridge to a sleepy Indian village where the only sound came from a school house; a teacher held up cards with letters of the alphabet on them, and the kids chorused the name of each letter. A few people rode by on horses.

On two other days, I hiked in the opposite direction through a jungly strip that divided cattle ranches from the river. I met Maya men who'd been hunting iguanas and carried them on poles. Another Maya named Eddie Xix (Shish) who was clearing bush with a machete, told me he was going to erect cabins for tourists on his family's land. When he indicated that his people had lived on the same piece of land since ancient times, I tried some names on him, of people and landmarks, from Caddy's journal.

Burrells Bank, Mudian Landing, Labouring Creek and Tiger Run; Mr. Forte, Mr. Turner, Potts "the ferryman," Dr. Young, "a gentleman of colour educated in England." These were places and people encountered by Caddy in the first week of his trip but none of them meant anything to Eddie Xix. Not only has the river changed its course innumerable times over the years, it hasn't for decades been used for transportation at all and, consequently, the old names are long forgotten. As for the plantation owners, it would take one of those dedicated local historians such as you do find in small towns throughout the world, to trace their passage and discover their counterparts. Maybe I'd come back and locate this person but there was no time now.

"Oh, yeah. There was one other man," I said to Eddie Xix. "He had some official titles in the city and a big plantation around here somewhere. Grew sugar cane but made his fortune as a mahogany cutter. Despite his wealth and his big house, he preferred to sleep in the bush. He was flamboyant..."

"That must be Usher," Eddie said.

"You've heard of him?" I exclaimed, in amazement.

"Oh, sure. Old man Usher's place was back there near the village where you were."

On November 18th, the fifth day of the expedition, Walker and Caddy, and their party stayed at Usher's plantation. When they arrived, the boss man was in the jungle, and a servant went to fetch him. Caddy describes Usher as he came galloping up on a "rough and ready nag," toting a rifle. He was "picturesque and brigandish" wearing a broad brimmed panama hat, red flannel shirt, white trousers, tanned leather mocassins; over his shoulder was a painted leather bag, "a sort of omnium gatherum;" from a wide belt around Usher's waist hung a machete, "or negro cutlass."

I continued walking to the pleasant little town of Succotz where there is a cable ferry at the narrowest point in the river. On the other side is a trail that leads to the relatively little known Mayan ruin of Xunantunich. I envisioned Walker and Caddy passing this spot on the river, unaware there was a smaller version of Palenque just half an hour through the jungle.

(As I discovered the following day, there is another ruin on the other side of the river, on private property. This site has not been excavated at all. The property owner introduced me to a Maya who lived on the grounds but had no interest in these ruins, Xunantunich,

Tikal or any other sites. The man told me the idea that his own ancestors were the builders of any of them is absurd. "These are not buildings done by Maya people." When I asked who was responsible, he pointed to the sky, said: "The people from out there.")

Five minutes from Xunantunich, I came to a full stop in the middle of the dirt road. I didn't move a muscle. Crossing the trail, ten feet in front of me was a four foot long brown snake with a squarish head and yellow markings. It had that special aura of menace that only certain snakes have. You instinctively freeze when you see a bushmaster, a coral snake or a fer de lance. The way you don't with a boa constrictor, say, or even a rattlesnake—to which the fer de lance is related.

There were two park rangers at Xunantunich, a black guy and a Maya. They became quite serious when I described the snake to them. Fer de lance, they agreed. A killer. "Did you apologize to the snake for looking its way?" the Indian asked me. When I said that I had not, he shook his head, "Well you will see Senor fer de lance again."

I didn't see the Senor on my way back so I put the man's prophesy out of mind.

After a few days along the river, Eddie Xix's dad gave me a ride to the Guatemala border. I shared a collectivo to Tikal with two English guys with bad haircuts called Tidwell and Fipps. They were pale and sweaty with red noses and sunburned strips along their forearms. They were from Bristol. Tidwell seemed to know a lot about Guatemala and Mayan archaeology and kept up a steady stream of commentary for Fipps' enlightment. Fipps apparently knew nothing about any of this and always looked on the verge of either weeping or passing out.

My friend Kevin Brown was waiting at Tikal. He's a world traveller with a diverse resume that includes union activity, crossing Afghanistan on foot, living in Goa, and making a film in the Slovak Republic. But his special interest is in Mayan culture. Tikal is his favorite site. We agree on most things but not about that. Tikal is the Guatemalan government's showpiece and more than a little tarted up, more than a little like a theme park. At dawn and in the early evenings, the steps of Temple Three are covered by ecotourists in Tilley attire, ooohing and aaahing over the sunset. I was put in mind of modern versions of the rigid figures on temple gylphs.

One gets a heavy dose of attitude from this kind of tourist, the dominant type, and you hear plenty of talk about the wondrous achievements of the holy Maya People. But the "people" lived on the plains below working the fields and never made it up to those plazas except to haul produce or when sacrifices were required. The occupants of those great buildings were the elite, an oligarchy of blood thirsty but brilliant monsters.

Another thing to bear in mind about the great grey limestone temples of Tikal, especially when someone is prosing about how it's possible to feel just how it was in the High Classic Period a millenium past, is that all these temples were a different colour back then, a more appropriate colour. They were all painted blood-red.

Kevin went home and I started across the western Peten.

"The road was exceedingly bad," Caddy wrote, in 1840, of the approach to the lake of Peten Itza. It still is.

The town of Flores is on an island out in the lake. Walker and Caddy were taken over in canoes. There is a dusty causeway now but caiman, Caddy called them crocodiles, still lurk in the mud and weeds along the shore.

There is a street that follows the perimeter of Flores. Steep laneways lead to the centre of the small island and the municipal buildings. The town looks like it should be the setting for some late-Thirties movie where Clark Gable blows into town in a pith helmet pretending to be a carefree adventurer but is actually on the trail of Conrad Veidt, the evil villain who wants to take a deadly plant back to the evil laboratories of Nazi Germany. Joan Crawford and Marlene Dietrich lurk in the streets and in saloons under ceiling fans.

When Caddy was passing his week in Flores, he witnessed a gang of blacks being led into town in handcuffs having tried to foment a local revolution. He was invited to a dance where the young single ladies advertised with their dowries in pouches around their necks.

Me, one morning I saw two young teenaged girls come running out of a house followed by a very old and drooling man with both hands extended before him, fingers wriggling.

Caddy left Flores, passed through the twin towns on the mainland shore, San Bonito and Santa Elena, reached the settlement of Sacpuy, and headed southwest to the Usamacinta River that separates Guatemala and Mexico. I made a decision not to be a purist, to leave Caddy's trail for awhile, after Sacpuy, and catch up to him in the State of Tabasco. My way lead directly west across the Peten to Naranjo on the San Pedro River. I did this because on neither of my two maps, each printed within the past few months, was there anything resembling a road. Some guidebooks indicate there is a trail, and even a bus that follows that trail, although they declare it to be too dangerous a route to pursue.

Actually, there are two buses to Naranjo. One of them leaves in the early morning from a station at the foot of the causeway on the mainland. Should a gringo or a well-off Guatemalan ever cross the western Peten, this is the bus he or she would most likely take. I reasoned, therefore, that it is the bus that is most likely to meet with trouble in the form of robbers or highjackers or worse. So, it is not the bus I took.

I rode the contraption that caters to workers, sharecroppers and villagers. It left from the market area of Santa Elena where raw sewage runs down the middle of the streets, a market that seemed like a meeting place for all the deformed of the area. There was a gaullimaufry of amputees, from people missing a single limb to double amputees to an armless, legless man in a box mounted on a tricycle pulled by a boy who seemed unusual for having no visible deformity. The cleaver strikes of an albino butcher barely disturbed the veil of insects around a slab of beef. A young woman in a satin skirt with paralyzed legs pulled herself through the filthy street on her hands.

By the time we left at nine-thirty in the morning, splattering shoppers and loiterers with grey stinking water, every seat was occupied and could have been occupied three times yet again by the people standing in the aisle. Most of the passengers were older Indians but there were many children and several young guys in military fatigue pants and sleeveless t-shirts. There was none of the feeling of menace or tawdriness familiar to anyone who has ever ridden a bus in America.

The shock came as we left the three towns behind. I had pictured the bus racketing along a jungle trail, palm fronds scraping against the sides, tickling the arms of those fortunate enough to have a window seat. There was jungle too but it was far back from the road, just visible beyond wide swaths that had been slashed and burned. And this was how it would be for most of the trip.

When I expressed my surprise, the guy next to me, named Henrique, said all this clearing of jungle land had happened in the past year. Until 1997, only a very few people lived in the entire Peten region (4% of the population) and most of them lived around Flores or to the north and east near the borders of the Yucatan and Belize.

I asked why the sudden change, and Henrique told me that the political situation was more liberal now than it has been for fifty years. The people had traditionally been afraid to venture into the western Peten, home to guerillas and the military who hunted them. The regular campesino was prey to both.

So political liberalization has brought with it devastation of the last large forested area in the country. Plantations are being developed and the land owners employ peasants who farm in the manner they have farmed for all times: slashing and burning before planting, and, after three years when the soil has been exhausted, moving on to slash and burn and plant elsewhere. The carbon inside the trees is released once they are set alight and enters the atmosphere as carbon dioxide. The soil erodes.

One environmental study I would later read predicted that all the forest in the Peten, the last in the country, would be gone by 2012. The study was naively optimistic, having been compiled before the recent devastation in the region. Ironically, "Guatemala" is a Nahuatl word meaning "Place of Forests."

Henrique told me that until a few months ago there had never even been logging in the area. The hardwood trade had flourished in the north and west but now the road brought loggers searching for mahogany. With no controls, entire hectares might be clearcut to take a single mahogany tree.

Later that afternoon, having covered eighty kilometres in five hours, I got off the bus with Henrique to go to his family's place a couple of hundred yards off the road, far enough away to be on the edge of the jungle. Henrique's people lived in three homes on pilings with roofs of palm thatch. The men spent all day with machetes and cans of kerosene destroying the jungle, then came home at night to tend their own little acre that had been burned a few months before. The women cooked and baked on outside fires and did the washing. A couple of girls maybe sixteen or seventeen were always around in short dresses, always shaking long thick black hair off their faces. I was put in mind of an Erskine Caldwell novel transposed to the tropics.

Henrique was the only one in the family to have gone all the way through school. He worked in an office in Santa Elena for a company that shipped what he called Xate to the United States and Europe. All I understood, until we went for a walk in the jungle, was that Xate was a plant. Because I have a special interest in palm trees, I recognized it immediately: a form of palm, chamaedorea elegans. You might have seen it at a funeral or in a floral arrangement.

"Next to hardwoods," Henrique said, "Xate is the biggest forest product."

He snapped four or five fronds from a tree that grew in the shadows of other trees. "We leave one stem so the plant can keep growing. We take Xate without destroying the forest."

I spent the night in a hammock in one of the thatched roof cottages and woke in the morning to strange jungle sounds and familiar ones of roosters crowing. Breakfast was eggs, beans, tortillas and thick sweet coffee.

Back on the bus in the afternoon, I sat next to a woman and her three grandchildren, girls five to ten years old. Between my feet, a piece of foam had been stuffed into a hole in the floor.

If the route to the San Pedro River underwent some massive improvement it might call to mind an abandoned B.C. logging road. But travelling it now is like a 200 kilometre journey over speed bumps. In these countries, the word for a hump in the road is Tope. I had a vision of the forest still shouldering the road and a "tope" sign on every tree, sort of a berserk version of Burma Shave.

An hour into the second day's trip I was surprised to see an actual patch of jungle near the road but an instant after I registered the thought, a black Toyota landcruiser catapulted from the jungle and blocked the bus. A loudspeaker was mounted on the roof from which a voice shouted, alternately in Mayan and Spanish. The passengers quickly became agitated. They weren't speaking Spanish, and I had no idea what they were saying. At first, I thought it was some kind of electioneering going on. Then some of them looked at me, gestured, pointed to the floor.

When I did not immediately catch on, one man took hold of the back of my head and pushed, telling me in Spanish to get down. I did, and the next thing I knew, a blanket was being thrown over me. I heard the grandmother say something to the little girls, and two of them sat on top of me, like they were sitting on their bundles in the aisle.

My face was so close to the piece of foam that I couldn't focus on it clearly. I could turn my head though, and looking right, up past a flap of towel, and to one side of a brown knee, saw, through the cracked bus window the heads of people with machine pistols and sten guns. One of them hoisted himself up for a look in the window. It was too crowded for anyone to get on and search the bus. I heard heavy footsteps on the roof and the disembodied loud speaker voice telling the people that they were helping to destroy the jungle which is their national heritage, warning them that they will have to pay for this devastation, one way or another.

After several minutes which seemed like several hours, the lecture ceased. The guys with the guns must have returned to their vehicle because I heard it move off, back into the woods, and our bus started up again. There was the lumbering of the motor and the screech and grind of the gears, and only after several minutes did they start lifting girls and blankets off of me.

People smiled at me, nodded.

"What did they want?" I asked.

"You," a young guy said.

I soon gathered that the purpose of these roadblocks was mainly to intimidate would-be settlers. But if there was anyone on the bus who had a little money to contribute to the cause, so much the better. I was told the bus rarely held a Guatemalan with money enough to steal, and never a gringo but the "eco-ladrones" (thieves) as one kid called them, always looked anyway.

Late in the afternoon we reached the end of the line, Naranjo which consisted of three buildings at a backwash of the San Pedro River. Two of the three buildings were saloons and I retired to one of them since no boatmen were leaving that day.

I wasn't halfway through the first rum when the waiter appeared with the second, holding it poised above the table while he asked me if I was a maricon (which is an impolite word for homosexual). When I told him I was not, he put the drink down and indicated a guy across the room.

He looked like a well-bred killer from somewhere in Latin America. I nodded and he came over to the table. Turned out he was, is, a well-bred killer from somewhere in Latin America by way of Luxembourg. Besides Spanish, Quiche and Nahuatl, he speaks nearly flawless French, German and English. I'll call him Astorias Baumann. He had spoken only to Indians for the last couple of months so he was eager to talk to me. I was eager to listen, and I did for two days. The man never said anything trivial.

We had a few drinks and he said he had to get back to his place before nightfall. He invited me to come along. We bumped along in his jeep over a series of diminishing paths until we came to a shack with a corral out back. Astorias spoke to a man in sandals whose brown feet looked like animals. The Indian saddled a couple of horses and we rode off.

"By the way," I said, "What exactly do you do back here in the jungle?"

"You'll see."

He told me some of the things he used to do. He had been taken to Europe as a kid and educated at private schools. After getting a master's degree in history, he joined the Legion.

"The French Foreign Legion?" I asked.

"Yes. But after five years there I signed up with the Spanish Foreign Legion."

I had never actually met anyone who'd served with the Spanish Legion but I knew that they thought of the French Legionnaires as sort of like the minor leagues.

He'd come to Guatemala at the behest of the military to train its elite troops, the Kaibiles, in jungle survival techniques. Baumann would parachute with three or four of them into the densest parts of the Peten. They'd hit the ground with a knife and an empty canteen and have to make do for two or more weeks.

"I quit in disgust after six months," Astorias said. "The usual policy was that for graduation a soldier jumped carrying a dog in his arms. After two weeks, he was supposed to kill and eat the dog. I refused to do anything to continue this barbarous custom, which is also quite unnecessary, and my superiors, all of them from the military academy, with no jungle experience whatsoever, and all of them sadists, made life difficult for me. So I just walked away. But I have stayed in this country."

A few minutes before we reached his camp, Astorias took a rifle from its saddlesheath, took aim at something I couldn't see and fired. Fired again. He sat still in the saddle for a full minute watching. I saw that the dark shape was a snake.

"Barba Amarilla," he said. "Luchesis lanceolatus."

"What's that?"

"You'd know it as fer de lance."

He climbed down and approached the seven–foot long snake cautiously, carrying a canvas tarp. Only after standing over the thing for another full minute, then prodding it with a stick, did he wrap up the fer de lance and sling it over his saddle.

So the Indian at Xunantunich was right, I would see the Senor again.

A few minutes later when we reached the house, I encountered a few of his brothers and sisters. It was a big house on pilings in a clearing. The roof overhung the porch on all four sides. Forming a swaying curtain on two sides of the porch were at least fifty snakeskins of all sizes, and when Astorias lit an oil lamp, I noticed that they were of all colours.

We went around the side of the house to a wooden contraption that resembled a tropical shower stall. Astorias apolo-gized for having to tend to business before we could get down to some serious yarning and rum drinking. He unwrapped the barba amarilla, hung it head first on a hook, and slit the monster straight down the middle of the stomach with a large fish knife. Next he scooped the entrails into a wooden bucket, covered it and washed the area.

"I'll take care of the rest later."

Over drinks he told me that I was fortunate to be seeing the western Peten just now for it is on the cusp—that's the word he used—of being transformed beyond recognition. It is a pivotal time. One year ago, he said, the area was the terra icognita just over the horizon. This year it is the frontier. Next year, there will be battles. Then, hell, maybe fences.

He hated to see nature's wildness be replaced by human wildness but it was inevitable. Anyway, Astorias said, the next couple of years, were going to bring him plenty of money—millions. And he didn't mean in quetzals. And he didn't mean in the snake business. He meant Mayan antiquities.

As people are penetrating the last forests, they are practically stumbling over artifacts. There may be, must be, ceremonial centres hidden in that vast forest track, entire Tikals and Palenques about to wake from their milennial slumber.

Astorias received reports from an entire network of huecheros—looters—with their own contacts among the peasants who cleared the brush. When the guys with the machetes found anything, they sold it for a few cruzeiros to a huechero who sold it to Astorias for a few dollars. Utilizing his international list of collectors, Asorias sold it for thousands, often hundreds of thousands. He had an extensive library of Mayan archaeology, a hundred books there in the jungle—none of which mentioned Caddy—and hundreds more at his apartment in the capital. He was on the internet too.

He had a few pieces around his shack. A couple of heads, a piece of a glyph tablet, and what appeared to be a miniature, two feet tall, stelae. For this, he said, he'd get four hundred thousand dollars from a man in Berlin. He was going to deliver it to Antigua in a week or so. Once the go-between, an archaeology professor, had the piece, he'd fax the collector in Berlin who would have the money transferred to one of Baumann's accounts.

He said he was trusting me not to rat him out. I could read the unspoken threat in his eyes. I'm not ratting him out here, and not only because this is a man who could walk blithely through a barroom of angry hockey enforcers without spilling his drink. I've changed details just enough to protect myself as well as the unwise and the sanctimonious.

The next morning I was surprised to wake up and see the snakeskin curtain. Hell, I was pleasantly surprised to wake up at all. I spent another day and night in the jungle, and we retraced our route back to Naranjo.

There we said goodbye, and I found a guy with a homemade boat to take me down the river. It was a sort of freighter canoe with an outboard motor and an awning in the middle. He was a Mexican in pointy boots and wide-brimmed hat who looked like he was about to step on stage and sing old Poco Sanchez songs. His teenaged son was the helper. He wore shorts, t-shirt and flipflops. There were three other passengers, a woman and two guys, who kept silent.

In half an hour, the boat pulled to shore and let off the woman who was met by a man, a child and a dog. The guys disappeared into the bush an hour later. As we got closer to Mexico, there were encampments of soldiers by the river. Just a handmade flag, a couple of tents and three or four young men with rifles. The captain steered toward shore so they could get a look at me.

The border was marked by a customs shed. We tied up at a floating dock and checked in; then I was lead across a field and through a patch of forest to a small army base. There were more papers to fill out and when I got back to the boat, discovered the customs official had boarded for a ride home.

Shortly after entering Mexico, we stopped again at a tin-roofed shack where four men were sitting on a porch. As we came up the trail, one of the guys got up and knocked eight coconuts from a tree. He and another guy lopped the ends off the fruits, like pale green footballs. I noticed each had their own way of wielding the machete.

One guy made compact vertical chops; the other guy had a looser touch, his angled ends being less precise. I got one of his. He handed it over with a smile.

A little later the jungle receded, the river was wide and still, a red sun was sinking and reflected on the water. Sky and water were indistinguishable, a line of jungle separating them. I lay back in the boat. Even the captain and his son, who must have made the trip hundreds of times, were quiet, as if it were sacrildegious to speak.

The calm was shattered as La Palma hoove into view, and a boat roared by with three laughing girls and a whooping white-haired man who waved at us, a beer in each hand. We followed him to the dock and when he saw me, there was no way I wasn't going to join the party. What party? I asked. The one I'll create, senor. And he did. It lasted until the morning. There was even a local cacique —chief—whose name was Geronimo, and everyone deferred to him.

The next night I was robbed.

The night after that I caught up with Caddy in Tenosique. His party had been greeted by barking dogs and a turnout of villagers curious to see some gringoes. Tenosique is a city now but still not used to gringoes. They stared. Near the hotel was a store that sold televisions. One was mounted outside on a pole and tuned to a boxing match. National hero Caesar Chavez was fighting in the capitol. By the time the bell rang for round one, a couple of hundred people were outside the television store. It reminded me of childhood in the Fifties in Philadelphia, crowds of people watching televisions in store windows when Rocky Marciano fought.

By the later rounds, the unthinkable had begun to happen. Not only was Chavez losing but losing to a non-Mexican. There was a different mood now on the street. As the only non-Mexican around, I thought it best to all of a sudden not be there.

The next day, I stepped down from a six passenger bus onto the streets of San Domingo de Palenque.

In January 1840, Caddy and Walker had encountered the

surly mayor of the place. The man's manner had not improved a few months later when Stephens and Catherwood arrived. Perhaps the mayor was simply part of a surly tradition which has continued to this day. The locals not only despise foreign visitors, they don't seem to like each other much either. This was the first place I'd been, this trip or any other trip to Mexico, where the looks were almost entirely hostile. Not even the clerks in shops that sold Sub-Commandante Marcos t-shirts relented.

I spent most of my time at the ruins fifteen kilometres away. I caught the bus across the street from where a Mexican man was lying on his stomach, drunk and unconscious on the sidewalk. Someone had pulled his pants down. As I was waiting for my bus, I saw a man go by with his son and spit a long stream of fruit juice across the drunk's naked buttocks. The little boy imitated his dad, and they laughed.

There is nothing tarted up about the Palenque ruins. They are vast and the jungle shoulders the buildings. You get the sense that should the maintenance crew take too long a lunch break, the jungle would reclaim its fabulous secret. Climbing the steep steps of the palaces and the Temple of Inscriptions, it is as if the cries of the howler monkeys are warning you to stay away. No groups loiter on the steps to pose and declaim the wonders of the proud Maya. There is a genuine feeling of awe.

Walker and Caddy were accompanied to the ruins by a Mexican called Don Juan. This man who would later serve Stephens and Catherwood, had also been with the legendary Count de Waldeck twenty years earlier. Waldeck is the one who drew strange dinosaur–type creatures at the ruins. Of all the visitors to Palenque, Waldeck was the most flamboyant. In fact, he is one of the great rogues of all time. His interest in antiquities had been inspired by his service with Napoleon in Egypt. He was over sixty by the time he reached Palenque although his life, incredibly, was little more than half over.

Scholars have always criticised Waldeck for the "inaccuracy" of his architectural drawings and the "fancifulness" of his landscape sketches. The "proof" of the former is that he got some of the proportions wrong; the latter is evidenced by those weird animals. No one has pointed out that here was an experienced artist—Napoleon never found fault—recording what he purported to see in a virtually unexplored wilderness. How does anyone know he didn't see dinosaur-like creatures, giant lizards, for instance?

(Waldeck died in Paris at the age of 111, tripping on the pavement as he turned to watch a pretty girl walk away.)

Waldeck was a man from another time. Stephens was his antithesis, a sober, serious, no-frills researcher. John Herbert Caddy was a sort of transition figure, linking the old and the new.

Caddy stayed for a couple of weeks drawing and writing in his journal. Then he and Walker continued on to Merida in the Yucatan. They arrived back in Belize City just as Stephens and Catherwood were reaching Palenque.

Walker produced a dry and uninspiring report which along with Caddy's finished drawings disappeared in the files of the Foreign Office.

Stephens wrote a book which was published in 1841 that included engravings from Catherwood's drawings. The two–volume work, Incidents of Travel in Central America, Chiapas and Yucatan has never been out of print.

Both Patrick Walker and Frederick Catherwood died by drowning. Stephens succumbed to malaria in Panama in 1852. John Herbert Caddy, resigned his commission in the late-1840's and returned to Canada, settling first near what would become London, Ontario where he helped draw the plans for the new city. He quit engineering work to teach art, and after a few years quit teaching to wander the southern Ontario countryside, drawing and painting. Caddy was the only one of the four to reach old age. He died prosperous in 1883.

He left few traces, this artist and adventurer. But his name is recorded inside one of the temples at Palenque. It is etched into ancient stone near those of Stephens and Catherwood, and the rest, but above them where it belongs: John H. Caddy.

Otherwise, it is as if the man never existed, as if the jungle of time and forgetting had swallowed up his story.

MORE ROADS

By the side of the road six miles out of Tuxtla that's where the Federales ran me down.

Leandro Martine

HALF-RUSSIAN

I was staring down at the sweep of the Tetsa River, remembering
the first time I had seen a wolf in the wild all those years ago. It
had been around here and from a bus window just like this.

Someone tapped me on the back, and I half turned my head.
"Watch when we go around the bend," the guy said. "Beautiful view,
Steamboat Mountain."

The old Indians called it that because it reminded them of the
white man's steamboats. The whites named the next big mountain
Indian Head.

"Wish I could paint that," said the guy.

Turning all the way, I saw someone who didn't look like
anyone's idea of a painter. He had a wide mouth, broken nose, black
eyes and a crescent scar on his forehead. He admitted having gotten
interested in art while in prison.

"There was an old Indian in there, a carver. He was real calm
in the middle of all the noise and hassles there in the joint. That
impressed me, his stillness. I asked if I could watch him work and he
let me. I watched him for months before I ever dared to touch a piece
of wood."

The guy told me his name was Arthur.

"I'm half-native, half-Russian."

He was going home to Whitehorse from Terrace. He'd recently lost his two year-old truck in a wager on a heavyweight fight.

"I was with my buddy. I didn't even want to bet against Foreman but neither did my buddy. So we flipped to see who'd bet Moorer. He was putting his Cougar up against my truck, 4 by 4, positraction. I lost the toss and lost the bet. Ah, we were all liquored up."

His buddy told him the next day to forget it, that the truck would be in the driveway waiting for him.

"So that's cool," I said. "He wasn't holding you to the bet, given the circumstances. Sounds like a good friend."

"He is but I can't take the truck back. It isn't right."

"You were both drunk, right? And it wasn't a real bet anyway. And since he's offered and you need the truck in the Yukon..."

"But, you see, the reason I can't take it back is because, deep down, I know if I had won, I would be driving the Cougar right now stead of riding this bus."

Arthur told how he happened to be in Terrace to begin with. The story began at a camp in Burwash in the Yukon where he was working. The camp was for geologists and prospectors. Arthur did some unspecified chores and lived in one of the cabins with his girlfriend. He was moving in on the incident that precipitated his departure but digressed, as do many good storytellers. His digression concerned an encounter with a grizzly. It seems some tourists had been around Burwash, asking directions to a certain hiking trail, and Arthur pointed them on their way. A few days later, the rest of the men from camp were in Whitehorse for r and r, and Arthur went out with his dog to patrol the area. A grizzly appeared and gave chase. The hikers had left garbage lying about, and the grizzly was hunting for more of the same. Arthur went up a tree and the bear kept him there. In the meantime, his dog tried its best to harass the grizzly, getting as close as possible, then hurrying away.

Finally, exasperated, the bear went off.

"When the guys got back from Whitehorse, I told about the bear and a couple of them went out and shot the thing. I wanted the claws for a mask that I was planning to make. I had to take a saw to the wrists. Those bones are so strong it took me nearly three hours to cut through them. Anyway, when the paws were off, I put them in a big pot to boil over the campfire. It was going to be awhile until I could separate the claws so I left the fire to tend to some other chores. When I got back, the pot was still on the fire and the water was boiling away but the paws and the claws were gone. I couldn't figure out what had happened until I found my dog who was acting real ashamed. Looking up at me, dragging his belly, you know, the way they do. He managed somehow to pull the paws out of the boiling water. I was angry but the damned dog had probably saved my life."

Arthur took a nearly full pint bottle of vodka from his coat pocket. "Have half," he insisted, holding it out to me. When I poured a shot or so into my empty coffee cup, he said, "No, no. We're partners. We have to divide it strictly in half."

He poured more into my cup, and took a sip from the bottle.

"One morning up there at Burwash, I had to take a geologist out in the bush. We were to be gone three days, two nights. Well the guy got lucky, found what he was after late on the first day. So we made camp and set out back to Burwash early in the morning. It was only about two in the afternoon when I got to the cabin. I went in and there was my woman in bed with one of the guys from the camp. I thought he was a friend of mine. He jumps out of bed and starts putting his clothes on. I guess he figured I might try and kill him, he'd heard stories about me. Meanwhile, she's looking terrified. The guy ran the hell out of there."

"What did you do?"

"I didn't do anything at first. Didn't say anything. Then I walked out and went straight to the pub. Had a drink or two, went back."

We both took a sip of vodka.

"And then..."

"And then when I got back, the place was all cleaned–up, bed made, dishes washed. She'd done the laundry too and even ironed my clothes and put them in piles. Shirts here, pants there, underwear. Ready to be put away. Up til that moment I didn't know what I was going to do. Didn't have a clue. But I saw the stuff piled there all clean and pressed, and I transferred all the laundry to my suitcase, got in the truck and drove away. Never said a word to her. Drove all the way to Terrace."

We had a stop at the Liard River. There was a Korean passenger I'd been talking to earlier. After I'd told him I was getting off the bus at Watson Lake, he tried to convince me to stay on til Whitehorse because we could both make money there. At Liard River, he showed me postcards he'd just purchased of the surrounding area, all summer scenes. He tugged at the sleeve of my parka. "You sure you no go to Whitehorse?"

"Positive, Jack."

"Oh! Hah, hah, hah!"

Arthur scowled at him. Back on board, he warned me, "Better watch out. I don't trust that guy. A lot of those Chinese guys are in a kind of Mafia they got, the Tongs, something like that."

Arthur told prison stories and about various altercations in which he'd participated. He was certainly the kind who attracted police attention and police harassment. He said he'd spent half his life in institutions. "Sometimes I even done the deed."

At other times, he swore he'd been innocent, and there were, admittedly, occasions when his bad actions went undetected. "So it all works out. Couple of summers ago I decided to try and sell my carvings and masks in Alaska. Figured there might be a better market over there. So I loaded my truck and took off. Got to Anchorage and was having a few drinks in a bar when these two Eskimo brothers start hassling me. They're mixed-up people, you know. Eskimos. Especially in Alaska. Many of them are inbred. First, these two begin ranking me for being Indian. Then it's: I'm a goddamned Indian from Canada. One said, 'What the fuck you doing in my country?' I said, 'I'm just selling my art. I don't want any trouble.' Then he repeated it, 'Fuck you doing in my country?' And I told him again but when he posed the question the third time, I said, 'Look, I'm not going to say it again.' 'Ah,you're not?' says the other one and grabs me. Then his brother was on me. I reached down and got the blade from my boot and stuck him. 'My brother,' the guy says. 'You stabbed my brother.'"

Arthur took off, into the truck and was gone.

We crossed into the Yukon at Contact Creek but a few kilometres later, the road dipped back into British Columbia. Arthur remembered two brothers, Indians, identical twins that he'd grown up around. "Their names were Byron and Shelley."

"No kidding?"

"Hey, I swear it."

Byron and Shelley had been frail, delicate little boys and were the same way as teenagers.

"They were a couple years younger than me, effeminate. When they were sixteen, they left the Yukon to go Outside where, I guess, they thought they'd feel more comfortable. Didn't see either of them for years. Then I'm in Okalla and, this one day, I see the twins. By now, these two were extremely effeminate, very pretty. When they come in there, a lot of the other guys are whistling, hollering what they're going to do to them. There were some other savages from home, and we decided we had to protect the twins. But they didn't want our protection. See, since they liked doing that kind of thing, they figured they'd have themselves a good time. But they'd never been inside before. We tried to tell them it wasn't going to be the way they pictured it. But they didn't listen. Soon there were lineups outside their cell. Byron and Shelley were in there sucking guys off and giving up their rears. But it soon turned rough. The kids didn't get any rest. The guards did them too. At night you could hear the twins whimpering, sobbing.

"Well, I got released and a few years pass and I'm in remand centre this one day and a little bent over fellow comes up, 'How ya doin, Arthur?' I asked him how he knew my name. He goes, 'Geez, don't you recognize me? It's Byron.'

"Even after he told me who he was and I'd stared at him, it still took me awhile. But it was Byron, all right. I swear he looked like an old man and he looked sick too, coughing all the time, his hands shaking. I asked him about Shelley, and he started to bawl. Shelley went and hanged himself in his cell at Okalla."

Arthur talked about being thrown in the hole, naked, cold, getting one bad meal a day. And this might go on for days or weeks at a time. From the hardship of prison, he progressed to the hardship of being "free." But he never really complained nor did he recite any litany of the obvious woes that were his to endure as a still-young Indian male, a scary-looking, still-young Indian male.

Reaching into his overcoat pocket again, Arthur brought out a thick rectangle of aluminum foil that he carefully unfolded. "What does this look like?"

"It looks, to tell the truth, like a bit of flesh with hair stuck to it. Hell, must be part of a scalp."

Arthur let loose with a yelp, followed by a fit of laughter. Glancing toward the front, I caught the bus driver's eyes in the big rearview mirror.

"Well, yes, indeed it does. Doesn't it?"

Arthur was in Prince George with a couple of days to wait for this bus to the Yukon. One night, he went into a bar and spotted "some savages from home." They waved him over to where they were sitting with two white guys. "One of the whites was good people," Arthur recalled, but "the other one was truculent from the beginning."

This guy began digging at Arthur.

"Everyone tried to ignore him. The other white fellow advised him to shut up. But the guy continued to stick little barbs in, all of them aimed at me. Finally, I said, 'What's bothering you, man?' He kept quiet for a few minutes then started in again and I told him to cool it. He said, 'Yeah, and if I don't what're you going to do, scalp me?'

"He stayed with that. 'You going to scalp me? You going on the warpath?' The others were embarrassed. Then when he got in my face with: 'Yeah, just try and scalp me!' I went, 'Okay, I will.'"

As he said this last, Arthur reached into his overcoat and came up with a hunting knife. His eyes flashed, his look hardened.

"So I grabbed a lock of the son-of-a-bitch's hair,"—he made a short upward pass with the blade—"and here it is."

Several strands of lank brown hair were still attached to an island of sickly pale skin speckled with dried blood.

"Know what I'm going to do with this?"

"No idea. Hang it from your belt?"

"Better. Going to make a mask that looks just like the punk, attach his hair and mail it to him."

We were back in the Yukon now and a few minutes later, at eleven thirty, there was the string of lights that meant Watson Lake. The bus rolled up to the depot in a service station-snack bar. There was an empty car outside with the motor running, of course; inside a woman could be seen opening up, switching on lights to greet the passengers for their forty-five minute layover.

Arthur and I trudged the other way, through the snow to the hotel, lifting our knees like cartoon Italian soldiers. I bought him a beer to make up for the vodka, and no sooner were we seated than we were joined by a guy I'd met twenty years earlier in Whitehorse. Arthur knew him too; a short, chunky and thoroughly bald man who used to help operate his father's drinking establishment before going outside to play hockey.

"I've been in this bar for three days and nights and you're the first guys I can relate to."

Immediately, he started to talk about his hockey career, how malevolent forces had conspired to prevent the success to which he was entitled.

Just a few minutes earlier we were on a bus rolling through the black northern night trading stories, now we were in the middle of a drunk's solipsistic maundering. His breath smelled like he'd spent all three days and nights eating sausage sticks from the box on the bar and those hardboiled eggs that floated in murky liquid in the huge jar that looked like it had been sitting by the cash register since the gold rush days.

Arthur tried to ignore the man, said something to me about carving, particularly about another native artist that he admired.

But the drunk had been listening.

"So you know Willie Joseph?"

"Yes."

"You a carver too?"

"Uh huh."

"You as good as him?"

"Maybe in twenty years. Why do you want to know?"

"Look, I own this condo in Palm Beach in Florida. If I had some good native carvings to sell down there I could make me and some natives rich. You interested in coming down there? Can you get Willie Joseph to come? I'll set you up in a place and you turn out some work. But, listen, eh?"

"Yeah?"

"You'd have to work hard."

The man couldn't focus his bleary eyes but he knew the order of things.

"Couldn't be drunk all the time."

He went on to let us know, or let Arthur know, that he was enlightened as hell when it came to relations between the races. He'd always dealt liberally with the innumerable drunken natives he'd encountered in his father's bar.

"I've been good to you people."

"You mean," Arthur said, staring hard at the man, "you've been good to Russian people or Indian people?"

"Huh?"

"Well," I said, getting up from the table. "Time for me to check into my room."

"A lot of Yukoners don't like your people. I'm not one of those kinds but..."

Arthur shot me a parting look, his lips twisted like he was suppressing laughter. I had a sudden flash of intuition, and knew what Arthur was trying to tell me. "Too bad this one's bald."

DOTTI, LOTTI AND THE

ICE-BLONDE BITCH

There I was last Sunday fighting the traffic on Highway 97, known as Harvey Avenue, as it creeps through the sprawling miasma that makes up Kelowna. Having spent an unfortunate year in that town, I knew that at night and from way up in the surrounding hills, high above the bowl of dirty air, the strip took on a hideous beauty, giving the illusion of a jewelled snake writhing through the night. But being on the ground was like being stuck in the beast's entrails.

I was trying to get to a vast flea market, a kilometre or so south of the strip. I wasn't idling my time, hunting for a bargain or junk to be converted into art assemblages. I was looking for a person called Dotti Day, an old acquaintance to whom I owed an apology. Back in '92 as I was spending those unfortunate months in Kelowna, Dotti told me a story that I had not only doubted but, frankly, considered to be a load of old nonsense. At first, after she'd spun the yarn and I'd gone away, the only thing I was curious about was why she thought I would have believed it.

208

Later I felt bad because this is not my way at all. I never dismiss another's story out of hand, no matter what it's about or how outrageous it may seem. Yet, after Dotti introduced her daughter and, later, explained the general circumstance of the girl's very existence, I did not believe her. In retrospect, my only excuse is that just about everyone else would scoff and even the most gullible might raise an eyebrow.

The flea market consisted of a large hall and an acre's worth of outdoor stalls. Just over the road is a vacant field and a substantial walled community of sand-coloured homes with salmon-pink roofs.

I had gone out there for art supplies which, that day, turned out to be a broken radio offered "as is," a small fish tank, two coffee tins of nuts, bolts and washers and a stuffed monkey. After making the outside rounds, I went in for a coffee and to browse in the used book section where, as usual, The Silver Chalice was fighting it out with Cavalcade of the North for most representation. Not finding any of the old surgery tomes that I collected, texts that make trepannation appear no more difficult than a build-your-own birdhouse handyman project, I happened to notice the long row of Harlequin Romances and stole a peek at one or two.

The covers featured bland, handsome young men and bland, attractive young women, exactly the type you see at tv auditions or up at Big White, the ski resort a few miles out of Kelowna. They were drinking deep of each other's eyes there among palms and frangipani, smouldering volcanoes in the background. It's taken for granted that romance blooms amidst tropical exotica or at those ski resorts with icing sugar snow. You never see any Harvey Avenues on those covers, let alone housing projects. But, in reality, romance can blossom anywhere.

"Yo, Jimbo! Looking for one you haven't read yet? Haw, haw, haw."

The speaker sounded like Vincent Gardenia with a cold in Deathwish. And she sort of looked like him too. Barely five-feet tall, with an incongruously large head, fleshy face, thin hooked nose, and dark, grey hair brushed back. She had on a green suede smoking jacket, green silk shirt, paisley ascot, charcoal grey trousers with a razor crease and high-sheen boxtoed black oxfords.

She extended a hand like a parrot claw. My old friend Dotti Day. It had been a long time, thirteen years at least.

With her was a girl as tall as she was but, as I found out, only twelve years old. The kid was dark-skinned with a long ponytail that reminded me of a brillo pad. She had on white runners, short pink socks with little pom poms at the back, black jeans tight on skinny legs, a jacket with a dozen zippers and a plastic parallelogram pin with the name of a band.

"Jimbo, I want you to meet my daughter Lotti."

Astonished, and hoping I was hiding it, I said the polite things and after a couple of moments, Lotti hooked into her Walkman, went out the door and took off on a mountain bike. No sooner had she pedalled away than I turned to Dotti who spoke before I could, "Yeah, yeah. My daughter. No shit. My honest-to-God darling little natural daughter. And you know the father."

"I do?"

The only guy we knew in common, as far as I could remember, was Marcel Horne who had introduced us. Marcel had been dead twelve years, since about the time I reckoned Lotti was born; it was possible, but Marcel was a white fellow.

It was Marcel, my best buddy, who had filled me with lore about the old-time Vancouver tenderloin. He was a firebreather and stage performer and had spent much more time in the carnivals than I had. In the winter, he'd work clubs like the Smilin' Buddha, the Delhi and the Shanghai Junk. But during carnival season, he was out on the road with sideshows, and he had once employed Dotti Day who lead him to an entire labour pool of half-men, half-women, always big attractions back then in places like Burns Lake, B.C. and Biggar, Saskatchewan.

"Marcel?"

"Don't be ridiculous. Hell, even if I was inclined that way, Marcel and I never spoke again after I took Ginger off him back in '72."

Marcel used to throw knives at Ginger or, rather, he threw knives around her perimeter, and she was his girl friend in a half-hearted way.

"So who is the father?"

"Jilly."

"Jilly! But—but..."

But Jilly, you see, is a woman.

"Yeah, Jilly. That big, sexy Swedish heiress."

We retired to Dotti's office so I could get the rest of the story in private.

"Yeah," she smirked, "all the afterhours clubs in all the world and that ice blonde bitch had to walk into mine."

Dotti'd run a joint in Gastown for the irrevocably lost and many who pretended to be. It had decent jazz too.

"After Lotti was born, Jilly stayed around for a few months but then her and her Maytag tongue beat it out of town. Yeah. It was bye-bye 'Couv; hello, Tangiers. Last I heard she was shacked up with some femme model married to a rock star. I've never trusted those double-barrelled broads but it's the kind I fall for. Like Ginger. Guess I figure they're just confused individuals whose minds I'm going to make up for them and they'll love me for it. But, on the other hand, if Jilly wasn't the way she was, and probably still is, then, Lotti wouldn't be here."

"Dotti, excuse me, but I think I'm missing the big part here. Jilly was a hundred percent woman, right?"

"One hundred percent, baby. No half and half that girl."

"Okay. So I guess you mean that Jilly is sort of the spiritual father, eh? Something like that. Wanting a kid, you went out, found a man...."

"No way! I mean, the thought of it actually disgusts the hell out of me. No offense. I only had sex, if that's what it was called, with a guy one time. One time. I was sixteen years old; figured I was supposed to try it. The only decent part was the cigarette after."

"So you must have had artificial ins..."

"Nope!" she cut me off. "Neither that or any other technique of modern science. Jilly is the fucking father I'm telling you. I got pregnant by her. So you don't believe it? Think how I felt when I went to the doctor cause I was feeling poorly and she said, 'Dotti, old girl, you're going to have a child'?"

So here's how it happened: Jilly, the tall Swede who stood to inherit a cool few million, though this certainly couldn't have mattered to Dotti, fell by Seymour Billiards on Seymour Street in Vancouver early one evening. There, she picked up a guy she later described, according to Dotti, as "some sort of Brazilian or something like that," and went back with him to his room for a little, again in Dotti's words, "hide the wienie."

Afterwards, Jilly jumped out of bed and hustled right over to Dotti's place. During the course of the usual passionate evening and Hindu love manual contortions, there occurred a transference of the Brazilian's still fresh semen from Jilly to Dotti.

Suspending disbelief for a moment, I mentioned the possibility that Jilly had been aware of the possible consequences and did the deed on purpose as some sort of sick joke.

"No," Dotti shook off the notion. "She was too dumb. Didn't use the jerk's washroom is all, just pulled on her panties and split, came waltzing into my apartment, flopped on the couch, hiked her skirt, gave me the old come hither look and crooked her finger, and as usual, Jimbo, I was out of my overalls in a New York minute."

I suppose I looked at Dotti incredulously because she shrugged, "Hey, you know, this sort of thing happens all the time. Well, maybe not all the time, you understand, but every now and again. My doctor gathered up references for me from the medical literature. I lost all of it a long time ago, but if you were of a mind and had a few extra minutes, you could look that stuff up too."

Later, as I was leaving, Dotti peeked inside my bag of junk. "A broken radio and a stuffed monkey. Geez, Jimbo, you're kind of unusual, you know that?"

And now I was back at the flea market three years later. This time Dotti was dressed less like Noel Coward and more like a truck driver.

"Dotti," I said. "I am humbled. Like you suggested back then, I looked it up. I went to the library, used the Medical Abstracts and found some pertinent articles. Most of them from that British medical journal, the *Lancet*. I got to tell you I was amazed by the number of precedents. In fact, there are enough to cause me to look over this flea market crowd and wonder how many of them might have been...well, you know. Anyway, I apologize sincerely. I should never have doubted you."

She smiled and then she slapped me on the back, "Hey, no problem, Jimbo, old buddy."

Dotti let me know the latest about her daughter. "Lotti's nearly fifteen now and she's got a boy friend. She's completely straight. I never pushed her one way or the other. But the guy, any guy, better treat her right or I'll take care of him real quick."

We hung around her office cutting up jackpots for an hour or so, and just before leaving, I said, "Dotti, why Kelowna? You?"

She sighed, "Ah, I know what you're thinking. But I've been here for years so it doesn't bore me as much as it did. What happened was I stayed in the city for awhile back then hoping against hope that Jilly'd come back. I suppose, I'll always carry a torch but I realized we were history. Then I started—now don't laugh or I'll bop you—I started going to church. It filled a hole, if you'll pardon the expression. I gave up staying out all night. You give up staying out all night and you discover Jesus, where do you go?"

"Kelowna?"

"Kelowna. Damn straight. But none of this means I've given up grappling with the same sex, eh? I don't suppose you know any nice clean Christian girls around here?"

I told her I did.

"How the hell do you happen to know a nice clean Christian girl?"

"Well it's a long story. But, never mind, she's not bent that way."

"Oh, well. If you meet one who is, be sure to send her around. See, I have this dream, I really do of..."

Dotti looked away and appeared to blush. She bit her lip.

"A dream of what?"

She pointed over the road, at the homes on the other side of the vacant field.

"A dream of settling down with that certain someone, maybe in a nice walled community kind of thing. Have barbecues. Grow roses. Be by each other's side forever. You think something like that's possible, Jimbo?"

"Yeah, Dotti. I guess anything's possible."

IT AIN'T O.K.

Brave, courageous and bold. Long live his fame and long live his glory. And long may his story be told.... Yes, he was some guy, Wyatt Earp. Some guy who killed my poor, defenceless 19-year-old Great-uncle Billy. And he would have killed my other great-uncle, Ike, who was unarmed at the time, there in Tombstone, Arizona more than 100 years ago, if he could have shot better. But the thing with Wyatt was, he had to be real close to kill you. It is a fact that Wyatt liked to sidle right up, usually accompanied by two or more brothers, and preferably when you had your back turned. Wyatt let off seven or eight shots at Ike, who was about 10 feet from him, and missed. Ike took it on the lam and survived what should have been called the Murders of Third and Fremont because that is the intersection where they occurred. But they've gone down in history as the Gunfight at the O.K. Corral.

You saw it, you saw all that at the true archive of history, the movies. Up there, beyond the heads, the hats, the popcorn outlines, unfolded the real story; there in that celluloid realm beyond Truth it existed, and exists yet: the living history. The murders near Third and Fremont streets are part of "your" history too. Don't give me any of that about being Canadian. You were formed by it, try as you may now to rectify the situation by hoping to turn up petrified bones in Saskatchewan, mildewed B.C. heroes or some outport outlaw. You had the chance and it's too late. Oh, plenty happened but you were looking somewhere else...And I think I just heard Gabriel Dumont murmuring assent from his moldering place. History is myth.

History is a lie.

A fact that keeps the professional historians working.

You had to have seen the film. They've been remaking it since 1932, and there're sure to be other ones soon. From *Law and Order*, with Walter Huston and Harry Carey, to *I Married Wyatt Earp*, starring Marie Osmond and Bruce Boxleitner. In between there has been *Frontier Marshall, Wichita, My Darling Clementine, Town Too Tough to Die, Gunfight at the O.K. Corral, Hour of the Gun, Doc...* (And several execrable entries to this sorry roster during the Nineties.)

Can't you still see it? Can't you see them coming down the dusty street, as ladies with parasols and bustles, ragamuffins, law-abiding citizens who all look like clerks scurry across the board sidewalks for cover? Four tough hombres doing a job they have to do but, of course, don't want to do. Silhouettes against the burning Arizona sun....

It doesn't snow much in that part of Arizona, but it was snowing that day. That may seem beside the point but it's an indication.

It is as if they have been taking that long walk down Fremont Street forever. (The O.K. Corral is still in Tombstone, but on Allen Street where it's always been. The next street over is Toughnut, where things really should have happened.) Randolph Scott, Joel McCrea, Burt Lancaster and James Garner (and Kevin Costner a serious example of miscasting) have had a try at playing Wyatt. His alcoholic, tubercular, lying, cutthroat, Georgia peckerwood, dentistry college graduate sidekick Doc Holliday has been interpreted by the likes of Kirk Douglas, Cesar Romero and Val Kilmer. Hugh O'Brien was

Wyatt in his tv incarnation. I used to think that he was the most ridiculous Wyatt of all (until Costner). Hugh O'Brien always looked as if he should be hanging around condo resorts in Boca Raton reeking of Brut and picking up middle-aged women or their daughters and selling underwater lots. But, then, that's what a contemporary Wyatt would probably be doing.

The most famous of the Tombstone movies was John Ford's "*My Darling Clementine.*" Like all the O.K. Corral movies, this one, although watchable, was a travesty. Ford claimed to have told the story according to historical fact with the facts coming straight from Wyatt Earp himself. Believing what Wyatt said was like putting your implicit trust in Baron Munchhausen. Actually, Ford got his information from the book "*Wyatt Earp, Frontier Marshall,*" by Stuart Lake. The old reprobate spent his last hours funning Lake, who may or may not have believed the stories but who, nevertheless, is responsible for the legend. From the pages of "*Frontier Marshall*" steps a man brave, courageous and bold indeed, a man born wearing a white hat. Only the most Simon-pure of actors could have played such a man in "*My Darling Clementine,*" and he did: Henry Fonda. The choice for Doc Holliday was a little harder to fathom: Victor Mature. Ward Bond and Tim Holt were brothers Virgil and Morgan Earp. Walter Brennan portrayed Newman Clanton, patriarch of the outlaw clan, but the actors who played his sons and their bad buddies, the McLaurys, aren't even mentioned in the cast list. Probably they were recruited from the ugliest guys of Gower Gulch, or maybe they plucked a bunch of winos off South Main Street in L.A. If Jack Elam had been around in those days, you could be sure he would have played one of my uncles.

My uncles.

At least I have the consolation of knowing that in John Sturges's 1957 "*Gunfight at the O.K. Corral,*" Uncle Ike was done proud by Lyle Bettger. I can remember seeing this movie at the Colonial Theatre in South Philadelphia and sensing even then that

217

something was wrong. But I didn't realize that those were my relatives up there preparing for Boot HIll. I only discovered that connection in 1981.

It was in the spring and I was with a pal, driving an old car up from Florida. We were passing through the town of Petersburg, Virginia, and decided to stop and pay a visit to my Aunt Louise. My friend and I were just a couple of drifters at this point, looking for something to happen. Coincidentally, we had both begun our wanderings in the state of Virginia, where he had grown up and where I was born. The Clantons also started their drifting from Virginia but I didn't know that at the time. I was going to find it out, though, in about five minutes.

There, drinking coffee at the kitchen table with my aunt Louise, was my mother. After the surprise, we took to reminiscing about my grandmother who had passed on two months earlier at the age of 95. "She left plenty of papers about the family history, all sorts of stuff about the Clantons," my mother announced.

"Who are they?"

"I declare! You know who I mean. The 'Clantons'."

"We're related to the Clantons?" I thought she meant Jimmy Clanton, the guy who sang "Venus in Blue Jeans."

She leaned across the table and whispered conspiratorily, "The outlaws. The O.K. Corral?"

"You're kidding? How come I never heard about any of this before?"

"You most certainly have. We've talked about it time and time again."

Perhaps it had been talked about during my childhood and I'd paid no attention. I didn't remind her that I'd been in Canada for the past thirteen years and most of what she said to me had to do with my staying out of trouble.

Then out came the proof, the monographs, excerpts from such obscure books as "*Guide to the Buildings of Surrey and the*

American Revolution," by James D. Kornwolf, extracts from family Bibles, histories of various branches of the family, even the wills of all these folks. I studied the genealogical records trying to pin down the exact relation. "Damn, Mom. A lot of them intermarried, didn't they?"

"Shhh!"

As far as I could figure, the father of Ike, Billy and forgotten Phineas, Walter Brennan or, rather, Newman Clanton, was my great-great-granddaddy. And in pouring through those family histories and reading the wills, many signed with an X, I discovered some very strange goings-on, particularly to do with slaves. But that's another story.

Soon I was digging up some of the popular accounts of the events in Tombstone, but all I got was confused. Naturally, I knew I had to go there. Had to find out at least something resembling the truth about what happened and who the actors were.

Travelling from Phoenix through Tucson to Tombstone is like retreating through the past 100 or so years of American history: from modern sunbelt America, sunbaked and despairing through the hopeful post-war forties boom time; to the Old West, surrounded by prairie vastness.

The bus station in Phoenix is patrolled by police, hips bulging with Magnums and clubs. A few blocks away the sidewalks of downtown are deserted and the sandstone skyscrapers sit like Saguaro cacti in a haze of exhaust fumes.

Downtown Tucson is Mexican territory and descendants of the old aristocracy walk the streets with cowboys and Chiricahua Apaches. I stroll into an old Wild West hotel with polished tile floor, marble-topped registration desk and wide, dark wooden stairs that swoop away in a sweeping curve. I half expect to see Katy Jurado slinking down the stairs, fingernails like weapons trailing along the bannisters. It could be 1947.

Climbing still higher to the plateau lands of eastern Arizona, there at the top of the rise is Boot Hill itself, markers stuck up among the desert rubble. Later I'd walk out and find the graves of Billy and Newman Clanton, the old man's plot ringed round by mesquite, like a crown of thorns.

Beyond was Tombstone, its board sidewalks and false-fronted buildings surrounded by mountains, the Dragoons, Mules, Whetstones and Huachucas like cutouts against a sky so dry and clear. Save for the cars and trucks, it cannot have changed much since 1881.

I was the only passenger to get off the late afternoon bus. The men really were leathery and lean, and wore boots to match. Their faces were burned to copper. I followed one of them into a bar.

The Crystal Palace. Swinging doors and wide planks floors, a mahogany bar, round wooden tables and a stage behind heavy curtains. The bartender was wracked by a cough to rival Doc Holliday's. Next door is the "Tombstone Epitaph" still in operation. A plaque noted that Morgan Earp was killed on that very corner in an ambush. I had to laugh. I had just read an essay about the West, the old and the new, by the well-respected critic and historian Wallace Stegner in which he asserted the old myths no longer have any relevance.

No relevance? To consider such a statement while drinking in a bar in Tombstone, Arizona, is a hilarious matter. It is to pretend those movies never existed. It is as if Fray Marcos de Naiz accompanied by his Apache Indians and Moorish slave, Esteban, did not in the year 1539 come out of old Mexico searching along the banks of the San Pedro River for the Seven Golden Cities of Cibola. As if Francisco Vazquez de Coronado did not arrive the very next year looking for gold and silver. As if the Indians and Mexicans and later the white men did not fight here among themselves across the centuries. And all of this long before that dedicated vagabond, Ed Schieffelin, discovered silver and created in 1877 a town on the very spot—as if in fulfilment of prophecy—where Naiz had envisioned the fabulous Seven Golden Cities of Cibola. When Schieffelin arrived in Arizona he was told by old-timers that his penchant for solitary prospecting would prove to be his tombstone, meaning the Indians would get him for sure.

So, establishing headquarters at a table in the Crystal Palace Saloon, I set out to deal with the legend of the O.K. Corral. More accurately, I threw myself against the wall of legend time after time but even the battering ram of truth couldn't dent the adobe or penetrate to the inner core of that story wherein resides historical truth. I should have known.

White outlaws had been in the area long before Tombstone was founded. Their principal occupation was making forays into Mexico to steal horses and cattle for sale to American ranchers. The silver strike simply meant a boom in the rustling business, since beef was needed to feed the miners. These outlaws were called "cowboys" by the "Epitaph" and they were led by Newman H. Clanton. His gang included sons Ike, Phineas and Billy as well as William Brocius Graham, alias Curly Bill, and one John Ringold, a cousin of the Younger brothers, known to history as Johnny Ringo. Another branch of the gang was centred around the McLaury ranch near Charleston, Arizona.

The Earps and their gang, led by Wyatt, were newcomers to Tombstone, arriving in 1879, after the silver strike. Wyatt was born in Monmouth, Illinois, in 1848 and went with his parents to San Bernardino, California. At the age of 20 he left California for Lamar, Missouri, where his brother Newton lived. When Newton announced he was going to seek election as sheriff, Wyatt, in a display of familial devotion, ran against him and won.

It must be remembered that in those days a job as sheriff or marshall really did amount to a license to steal. When Wyatt had taken all he could from Lamar, Missouri, he drifted to Kansas and supported himself hunting buffalo, which was against the terms of the Indian treaty. Arriving in Wichita in 1875, he was a cardsharp until gaining employment as a cop, from which position he was fired after his arrest for disturbing the peace. In Dodge City Wyatt was arrested for beating up a dance-hall girl and the next week became the assistant deacon of the United Church. In Dodge he was a gambler, usually stationed at the Long Branch Saloon, owned by Luke Short, who became one of his best friends. It was in Dodge that Wyatt acquired his other two boon companions, Bat Masterson and Doc Holliday. When Materson lost his bid for reelection as sheriff, the Earp brothers, Buckskin Frank Leslie, Wyatt's girlfriend Mattie Blaylock, Holliday and his pal Big Nose Kate Elder all took off for Tombstone.

The idea was to take over the town, to control the badges and the gambling. Wyatt immediately got himself appointed deputy sheriff, a job people killed for, since that official got to keep a large percentage of the taxes he collected and could collect them however he might. But Wyatt's zeal was too much even for a Wild West boomtown and he was fired. His replacement was one John Behan and here begins one of the feuds that would culminate in the murders of Third and Fremont streets.

Wyatt took a job as bouncer at the Oriental Saloon and got Morgan, Luke Short and Buckskin Frank in there dealing faro. Soon Virgil Earp was defeated for the city marshall's job by Ben Sippy. In January 1881, just when things were looking their bleakest for the Earp gang, came the incorporation of Cochise County. The first slate of county officials would be named by the governor of the territory. The Earps were Republicans, Governor Charles Fremont was a Republican and the mayor of Tomstone, John Clum, who supported Wyatt for sheriff, was a Republican. Ninety percent of the residents of Tombstone were Democrats, however, and Fremont appointed one of their number, John Behan, as sheriff.

Wyatt was furious. The job was worth $40,000 to him in tax commissions and he had lost out once more to Behan. Events now proceed rapidly, just like in one of those movies, the pages of the calendar flipping away in the winds of time against a background of gunfire and thundering hooves.

A Wells Fargo stage was robbed of $25,000 in silver. A posse comitatus of Wyatt, Virgil, Morgan and other gang members as well as Behan and his deputy tracked one of the robbers, Luther King, to a ranch owned by friends of the Clantons. King squealed on three accomplices: Jim Crane, Harry Head and Bill Leonard. Curiosity was aroused by the vigilance with which the Earps set out after the alleged robbers. Word began circulating that Doc Holliday had been with the robbers and that it was he who had shot and killed Bud Philpot, the driver of the stage. Also, Leonard was known to be a close friend of Holliday, whose presence could not be accounted for. Furthermore, it was common knowledge that Wyatt had worked for Wells Fargo and maintained contacts who could advise him of silver-bearing shipments. Then, curiously, Short and Masterson split town. Wyatt was spending all his time searching for Crane, Head and Leonard, hoping to kill them before they could talk. Somebody else did the job for him, though, in New Mexico where they had tried to rob a store. Not knowing this, however, Wyatt went to Ike Clanton, regarded as the baddest of the cowboys, and offered him $2,000 a head to kill the supposed robbers. Clanton refused.

Kate Elder, who had been living with Holliday, signed an affidavit stating Holliday had admitted to her the killing of Bud Philpot. Holliday was promptly picked up but released by Judge Wells Spicer, a friend of the Earps and, like them, a member of the Republican law and order group. At the hearing Ike Clanton testified not only that Wyatt had offered him a deal, but that Holliday had bragged to him about killing Philpot. The defence produced several witnesses to swear Holliday was with them and, as for Kate, it maintained she was drunk when filling out the affidavit.

Holliday was released and two days later Virgil arrested Kate for drunk and disorderly. When she got out of jail, he did it again. Kate left town.

As the summer days fluttered away, the action stepped up. The bad feelings between Wyatt and Sheriff Behan were exacerbated by their rivalry over a 17-year old prostitute. Several more Wells Fargo robberies occurred and it was noted that a member of the Earp family decided to visit his parents in California after each one. In August of 1881, Old Man Clanton was shot and killed by Federales, supposedly in retaliation for a raid on a pack train of Mexican smugglers. Upon hearing of the patriarch's death, Wyatt wasted no time in trying to take advantage of this ebb in the Clanton gang's reputation. He approached Ike with another deal, a fake stage robbery this time. Wyatt would inform Ike of the next silver shipment, which a few expendable members of the Clanton gang would try to steal. But there would be Wyatt and Doc waiting to come to the rescue. Ike Clanton would be a rich man and the Earp name would be cleared. Ike made the mistake of saying no.

Millions of words have been written about what happened on October 25 and 26, 1881. Here are a few facts. On the twenty-fifth, Ike and Tom McLaury went into town to collect a debt from Bauer's Meat Market and to get supplies. When the owner was not to be found, the men took separate hotel rooms and went out on the town. That evening Ike got into a poker game with Sheriff Behan and Virgil Earp. Bad words were exchanged. In the morning Virgil found Ike packing his guns and arrested him. After taking away his revolver, Virgil hit Ike over the head several times with the barrel of his rifle. At about the same time Wyatt accosted the unarmed Tom McLaury and gave him the butt of his rifle in the face.

After paying a $25 fine, Ike Clanton collected his money at the meat store and readied himself to leave Tombstone. Ike and Tom McLaury were 20 steps from the shop when Billy Clanton and Frank McLaury rode up. They had come in from the ranch to find out why the men hadn't returned. While the two pairs of brothers were talking, Sheriff Behan appeared to tell them trouble was brewing and to either hand over their guns or get out of town. They replied they were about to leave and didn't want any trouble. Behan went back to the Earp faction and told them to keep away. As Behan would later testify, "They paid no attention to what I said."

Morgan, Virgil, Wyatt and Doc pushed Behan aside and headed into history. Instead of that fabled long, sun-scorched walk, they cut through the alleyway between the O.K. Corral and Fly's Photography Studio and stepped out into the cold wind whipping down Fremont Street.

Now what is truly incredible upon reading the testimony produced at the O.K. Corral inquest, and recently made public by the diligence of Alford E. Turner of Tombstone, is that all the witnesses other than the Earps and Doc Holliday agree on what transpired. This includes not only Ike Clanton and his sympathizers but also his enemies, those who had no opinion of him one way or another, and people who had never laid eyes on him before. Everybody. And the whole affair was observed by a score of locals.

Now bear in mind that neither Tom McLaury nor Ike Clanton was armed, Frank McLaury was holding the bridle of his horse, and Billy Clanton had his hands in his pockets. Virgil, Wyatt and Morgan came out of the alley with their revolvers drawn and Doc produced a sawed-off shotgun from under his sheepskin coat. Upon seeing them, Tom McLaury held aside the flaps of his coat to show he was unarmed. Billy put his hands in the air. Frank continued to hold the reins of his horse. Wyatt, standing three feet from Billy, said, "You sons of bitches!"

Virgil hollered, "You've been looking for a fight!"

Instantaneously Morgan and Doc started shooting. A split second later Virgil and Wyatt opened fire.

Frank McLaury was killed before he had a chance to release the reins of his horse. Tom, unarmed, tried frantically to get out of the range of fire but was gunned down. Billy took three bullets at what they call point-blank range, fell to the ground, was hit again and, bracing his gun against his knee while lying on his back on the ground, wounded Virgil and Morgan. Holliday finished him off with a blast from the shotgun. Meanwhile seven or eight shots had failed to hit Ike, who stumbled into Fly's studio and rushed out the back door into Allen Street. Later, when the mythologizers got hold of him, Ike would become known as the "the man who ran away from the gunfight at the O.K. Corral."

It all took 40 seconds. But it was all just beginning.

The movies never indicated that sentiment in Tombstone was almost totally with the cowboys. The Earps barricaded themselves in Virgil's house until the next day, when warrants were obtained for their arrest along with Holliday's. There followed an inquest that lasted until a verdict was handed down December 1. The judge found the evidence to be insufficient to hold the defendants for trial and they were released. The editor of the "*Tombstone Epitaph*" wrote, "In the eye of many the Justice does not stand like Caesar's wife, 'Not only virtuous but above suspicion.'"

The judge was that old friend of the Earps, Wells Spicer.

As the bodies of Frank and Tom McLaury and Billy Clanton were carried through the streets to Boot Hill, local residents draped a banner over the coffins. It read, "Murdered in the Streets of Tombstone."

There were footnotes. Virgil was wounded again by parties unknown. Morgan was ambushed and killed outside the Crystal Palace. At the Tucson train station, while escorting Morgan's body to California, Wyatt killed a man whom he suspected of being the gunman. The Earps never returned to Tombstone.

Ike Clanton was shot in the back in 1887 in Bonita Creek, Arizona, by a deputy sheriff named J.V. Brighton. This character had completed a mail-order private detective course back in Indiana the year before. When he murdered Ike, he was wearing the tin badge that came with the course for 25 cents extra. On his person was the warrant for Ike's arrest that faintness of heart had prohibited him from serving.

And Wyatt. Wyatt continued roaming the West, getting into one scrape after another. In 1896 in San Francisco he refereed the Bob

Fitzsimmons-Tom Sharkey fight for the heavyweight championship. As the local paper had it, "Fitz was winning easily when Wyatt stopped the fight and gave it to Sharkey on a foul. It is agreed by boxing experts that there was no foul."

An inquiry revealed that Wyatt had bet heavily on Sharkey.

Wyatt escaped his bad press by going to Dawson City and later to Nome, Alaska. In 1911, recently released on a vagrancy charge, he was prosecuted in Los Angeles for fleecing a businessman in a bunco game. In his last years he sought pathetically to interest people in the story of his life. For a time he patronized the movies' first two-gun hero, William S. Hart. Finally he found Stuart Lake and the rest, if you'll pardon the expression, is history.

Wyatt died on January 3, 1929, and was buried at the Hills of Eternity Memorial Park in Colma, California. The night he was laid to rest thieves broke into the cemetery and stole his tombstone.

So that old bitch goddess Legend has favoured Wyatt Earp and spurned Ike and Billy as a couple of dirty saddle tramps. No biographers have come forth to tell their story. They have not been bathed in celluloid glory. And perhaps that is as it should be. History is just doings its stuff again.

Alford E. Turner is the world's foremost authority on these matters. His hair is snow white, eyes a startling blue surrounded as they are by a copper face cracked like the riverbed of the San Pedro in July. A thoughtful man, judicious, he knows the facts in all of this yet even he leans towards the Earps. Nevertheless, Alford told me about a relative of mine, Red Clanton, who was still around, 70 years old and a chuck wagon cook at a nearby ranch. We went looking for him of an evening but found him not very communicative. Old Red was lying blind drunk in the bunkhouse, snuggled up with a bottle of Jim Beam. We managed to make a vow to go and get us an Earp, any Earp.

And it is only in Tombstone that the name Clanton will get you anything. Mainly what it will get you is free drinks. In

Tombstone, you see, they know who the good guys were. My last night in town I'm at my usual table in the Crystal Palace when one of the barmaids approaches, points out some grinnng middle-aged individual with a camera around his neck and leads me over to the bar. The man announces that he is from Germany and proceeds to position the waitress and me the way he wants us.

"Yes, yes, goot," he says after snapping a few pictures. Then he has the waitress take one of him and me together, his arm thrown over my shoulder.

When he has all his shots, he thanks me. "You related to the Clantons so waitress tells me that. Old Man Clanton what is your relation to him, please?"

"Why, Old Newman was my great-great-granddaddy."

"That is wonderful, yes. This famous wild western town. I come all the way from Hamburg to see this."

"You came to the right place, pal. Everything happened here. Now take the word bronco, for instance. Did you know that word actually comes from the name of a countryman of yours? Had a mine here. Name of Brunckow."

"Oh, I shall write that name down."

"Do that. And look right here. Where we're standing in this very same spot, a famous expression, one that sums up everything, came into being. And I know you've heard it. Right at that very table there, one of Tombstone's most famous gamblers, Marcus Aurelius Smith, was involved in a faro game and, drunk at the time, was being taken advantage of by a couple of wandering cardsharps. A friend leans over and whispers in his ear, 'Get out of it, Mark. The game's rigged.'

"'So what!' snapped Old Marcus.

"'You're being taken, that's what.'

"'Hell, I know that, pal. But it's the only game in town, ain't it?'"

"Yah," nodded the man from Hamburg. "'The only game in town.' I like that."

THE RELIC

She was standing by the side of the road with her thumb out on Highway One near Cape Campbell. Deeply tanned, short, brassy hair stuck to her skull; she was over fifty for sure, and obviously a woman for whom the ozone layer was of little concern.

The breeze played with the hem of her cotton dress showing a bit of brown leg above the knee. She was too tough to be called thin or skinny, wiry was more like it. There was a cluster of fifteen foot high flax plants behind her, the tops like sword points piercing a pale blue sky.

I was in heavy traffic headed for the ferry and wasn't able to stop but I passed by so close that her gaunt face with deepset eyes seemed to fill the window. Her expression was almost pleading. In the sideview mirror, I noticed her poor old-fashioned suitcase in the gravel.

I was completing a circuit of the South Island, having gotten a lift with a seventy year old woman bush pilot to a lodge in Abel Tasman Park, earned my keep working on a barge, then drove along the wild Indian Ocean coast to Greymouth, caught the TranzAlpine train to Christchurch, headed down to Dunedin and Bluff, and returned.

I got the ferry over to Wellington but didn't see the woman on board.

I saw her a week later in the Wentworth Valley, near the town of Whangemata, her thumb in the air, suitcase at her feet. This time I eased to a stop on the shoulder of the two lane highway. She hustled over to the car, breathing heavily, and got in muttering broken phrases: "Hot...much obliged...Thanks....so bloody, um....Just let me...."

Her forehead was damp, there were beads of sweat on her upper lip and her short unusual coloured hair was still plastered to her bony skull. She closed her eyes, rested her head against the seat and took deep breaths as I pulled back onto the road. Despite her tan there was only a bit of crepe paper at the base of her neck. The hem of her dress had ridden halfway up thighs, her knees were wider than what came next.

She opened her eyes, saw me looking, twisted her face into a parody of being put upon and with an exaggerated tug at her hem, giggled. "Maybe if the German gentleman back there at the Nickel Strasse had gotten a look at me legs, I'd have gotten the job. But, no, the hausfrau never left his side."

I mentioned that I had seen her thumbing a ride to the ferry. She said that she remembered me, seeing my face in the window.

"Pity, you didn't give me a lift. Who knows we might have had a shipboard romance, a sweet idle hour before going our separate ways."

"Yeah, maybe," I said.

She had an English accent. Middle class. London probably. She told me she lived in Christchurch and was looking for a job. She'd been going to all the resorts putting in applications.

Just as I was wondering why she was hitchhiking she said, "I'm on a strict budget. Not a fucking farthing to spare.'"

"What kinds of jobs are you applying for?"

"Anything. Waitress. Busperson. Charperson. But, really,

dahling, who wants to be served by a scrawny, 55 year old broad when one is on one's holidays? I understand that. What galls me though is that they refused me the lordly job of changing sheets and cleaning toilets because of my age. Though I'm tough as nails. Don't I look capable?"

I glanced at her, "Yes, you certainly look capable."

"Thank you. I could say the same about you."

We drove in silence for half a minute before she asked me if I'd consider marrying her.

"I beg your pardon?"

"Well I feel rather ashamed coming right out and asking you like this."

Before I could reply that she ought to feel rather ashamed, she had switched to a lower class Scots accent and was saying she knew that I didn't love her.

"I don't have much hope left, you see. I'd be a good and dutiful wife, and loyal too."

"Well you better be," I told her.

She hiked her skirt back to the midway point, fluttered her lashes.

"And I'd see to all the rest of me wifely duties." She laughed and returned to her regular accent.

"It's the Victorian era. I'm a Scottish governess, an old maid running out of time. I'm desperate, don't you know. Desperate for someone to care for and have care for me, if only a little. I'll settle for scraps. I'll even settle for you, an old drunk."

"Typecasting!" By the time, we pulled up to the place at Tairua, she had me practically in tears with her recitation.

"Where's it from?"

"N.C. Hunter's, *A Day by the Sea*."

This was a resort by the sea with a restaurant and lounge. A sparse woods on a rise of land screened A frame cottages beyond which trails lead down through sand dunes to a bay of green water. I had a cup of tea while the lady tried to convince them to give her a job. She disappeared into the back with the woman who owned the place and a chef who might have been Spanish.

Twenty minutes later she appeared looking angry, jaw clenched, muscles quivering along her cheeks. She darted her eyes at me and kept walking toward the door. I paid and got out of there.

She was waiting in the car with her arms folded.

"The fat pig," she said, staring straight ahead, "indicated not too subtly that a certain sexual favour granted by me would do much for my prospects of obtaining a job washing dishes."

She turned to look at me, "No."

"No, what?"

"No, I didn't grant him that favour."

"Okay."

"I know that is what you were wondering."

"Come on, give me a break."

The next stop was a place near Whitianga. Her mood had improved by the time we got back on to the highway.

She told me she had come to New Zealand in the late Seventies.

"I had done plenty of theatre in London and some television. I thought I had a career in the works but then I thought I had fallen in love. With a damned Kiwi. He was being transferred home and like a fool I said Yes, and moved back with him. Auckland at first. Naturally, I attempted to break into theatre there, what little of it there was. But he was having none of it. Put his big foot down. Absolutely forbade it. Tell me, would you make your wife quit the theatre and get a regular job?"

"Hell, no. I'd make her quit her job and walk the boards."

"You, I should have married." She looked at me coquettishly, giving a playful once over. "Yes, I could see us married, living happily ever after."

"I got a wife."

"Oh, well."

"Wherever she is."

"You could get a proxy divorce and we'll grow old together. Or older."

"Sure thing."

"'When our grave is broke up again
And he that digs it spies
A bracelet of bright hair about the bone,
Will he not let us alone,
And think that there a loving couple lies'
"Da da da da da da da da and
'He that digs us up will bring
Us to the bishop and the king
To make us relics; then
I shalt be a Mary Magdalen, and you
A something else thereby.'"

"That's me," I said. "A something else thereby."

"Wager you don't know who that's by."

"Wager I do. John Donne."

"My, my. He has unplumbed depths."

"You're not kidding."

"Think of the life we could live. Bantering away in the parlour, while I do my knitting and you catch up on the football results."

"Yes, that's me, all right. I'm mad for the football results. Not to mention rugby. Not too big on curling though."

"Nineteen seventy-eight. I was a fine young piece back then though you probably can't believe such a thing. They were holding auditions for a television show produced right there in Auckland. They needed a spunky female with a nice little figure—suspend your disbelief please—and an English accent to hand out the prizes. I never told my husband that I went for an audition and then a call back and lo and behold I got the part. I was overjoyed. But he wouldn't let me go through with it, the bastard. The big bloody bastard."

She began to cry. After a minute she sniffed and wiped her eyes, wiped her nose.

"So sorry. Strike that. Forget it happened. I'm all right now. Here, here. Let's move on to other things." She had divorced the man three years ago but found herself stuck in Christchurch.

"A beautiful little city," I said.

"Certainly, if you're not hard up against it."

"None of them are so great then."

The man had vanished, leaving her nothing.

"I put a year in serving drinks in a pub but they let me go, saying they had to have a younger person since the old guard was moving on and their clientele was getting younger. There followed a stint as a waitress in a Malaysian restaurant. That lasted seven months until a cousin arrived from back home."

She stuffed envelopes, answered phones. Then it was the dole. But she didn't want to be on the dole.

"I'm full of vim and vigour," she assured me and I believed her. "Most of the time, anyway. But sometimes I just get so low. What's a girl to do?"

We had a picnic on one side of a little bay. On the other side, we could see the resort, the one in Whitianga where she soon would be putting in another application

"I consider myself a resolute little old broad. I can make friends with people. I like most of them, or can act like I do. I'm not stupid. So, I sometimes ask myself, what is the matter with me. There must be something the matter. Of course, I put away any dreams of acting decades ago, so that's not holding me back. I mean, I don't appear as if I'm too good to stuff envelopes or make beds. What happens to me in five years when I turn sixty? I try to picture myself at seventy and it ain't pretty. I just don't want to be a bitter and penurious old lady."

I replied to all this, of course. But it was just words.

Later, we got back into the car and headed for the resort. There was a long driveway, hard earth on either side of humped grass that wound its way to the entrance. The grounds were planted with tea trees and fifty foot tall Nikau palms whose tops looked like badminton shuttle cocks.

"Well that must be it," she said as the main lodge came into view.

"I've enjoyed talking with you," I said.

"And I you. Would you pull over, please."

There was a table under some trees at the side of the drive.

"I'd prefer to walk the rest of the way." I stopped the car. She reached over and turned the motor off. She took a deep breath.

"Well?" she said.

"Well what?" She glanced at my crotch, looked back.

"Aren't you going to ask me to earn my ride?"

"No. You already earned your ride."

She bit her lip, and closed her eyes but when she opened them again she was smiling.

"Here's some more of that poem. 'All women shall adore us, and some men...And since at such time miracles are sought....I would have that age by this paper taught....What miracles we harmless lovers wrought.'"

She got out of the car and, got her suitcase out of the backseat. The slamming of the door got the attention of a portly gentleman who was walking amongst the trees. He had on shorts, a golf hat and a cotton shirt with an alligator on the chest.

"'First we loved well and faithfully,'" she spoke to the man and jerked her thumb back at me like she was still hitchhiking.

"'Yet knew not what we loved, nor why...Difference of sex no more we knew...Than our guardian angels do...'

"Oh, you're no fun," she said to the man who just stood there with a vacant expression. And she turned again to me, "'Coming and going, we....Perchance might kiss....'" She leaned forward and kissed me on the mouth. She put a lot of effort into it and when she pulled back, her eyes were wet. She stared for a moment, then turned away with an exaggerated shake of her head which would have set her flowing locks in motion if she'd had flowing locks.

The wiry little woman walked toward the entrance swinging her cheap suitcase. The man in the golf cap said something to her but she never looked, just gave him the finger.

But she wasn't all that tough.

SAM SPRY

I t was not his incredible face that got my attention but the getup, his clothes being just so different from what you saw on the men folk of Beaumont, Texas.

Strolling that main stem—it's been more than thirty years—a street filled with trucks and cars and citizens on a Friday afternoon, what I noticed was a man in an Hawaiian shirt, long grey-blond hair nearly to his shoulders, who was leaning against a brick wall smoking a black stogie. His chino pants were baggy, shoes of woven strands of soft leather. He might have looked inconspicuous catching a smoke in Panama or Paramaraibo but you knew the guy wasn't local. I stepped off the curb and headed over.

He made your ordinary weather-beaten types seem like shoe clerks in windowless basement stores. Dimes could have been hidden in the furrows of his brow. That nose might have started out like Barrymore's but it took a few detours. His eyes were blue slivers of glass; lids walnut shells; one brow was split; and he was missing an ear lob.

But the guy had an ironic twinkle, an expression that reminded me of cowboy actor Ben Johnson just before he rode out to scout Indian Territory in "She Wore a Yellow Ribbon."

I had arrived in Beaumont just that morning, having come up from below the border. Floyd Wallace drifted in after signing off a ship at New Orleans. Since hitting town the week before, he'd headed up a crew that was framing a house in town. One fellow had quit and Floyd offered me the job.

He was staying in a rooming house and ostensibly had his own quarters but I'm pretty sure he spent the nights with the woman who owned the place. Floyd had known her late husband who'd been a railroad worker. Wherever we landed there was: 'Someone here we ought to look up.'

The framing job lasted another week and a half, after which we rode north in a caboose, courtesy of one of his contacts. The trainmen not only treated Floyd with the utmost respect, like he was one of them, which was curious enough, but they seemed to defer to him as well. He sat with those men on the benches drinking coffee from tin cups and slinging around all that railroad lingo about snakes and shacks, keys and ops and 4-8-4's. He gave the impression of being thoroughly knowledgeable about railroading, same as he'd done with construction work and as later I'd hear him discuss fixing boats and riding horses. But he was never boastful or overbearing.

We had enough money to fly out of there first class but that would have violated the principle of the enterprise, and we never would have met those great trainmen. Just turned twenty, I marvelled at the fact that this "old man"—in his late-fifties—was still seeking adventure.

We certainly had plenty of that both before and after pulling into Oklahoma City where, this particular afternoon, we were waiting in the relentless sun outside the door of a small house in a working class neighbourhood. Dry strips of paint curled like yellow woodshavings from the shutters, there was a rolled up newspaper gone the colour of urine on the concrete landing.

"Must not be home," I ventured. It had been a full minute since we'd knocked. In the driveway between houses, three men drinking beer at the rear of a pickup truck with the confederate flag in the back window, gave us the kind of looks they always gave people not like them.

"He's home," Floyd said, and I thought, 'How the hell do you know?' But, on the other hand, three weeks of knocking around with him had revealed the wisdom of accepting the guy's word.

The door opened on a man hanging from a pair of brass rails, the tails of his denim shirt brushing the floor. It was half a man with a big head and wiry salt-and-pepper hair.

He gaped at Floyd with surprise and astonishment, and glanced at me for a split second before turning his attention back to my partner. "Why Greeley! You ugly old so and so!"

"Sam Spry, you ain't dead yet!"

"No, I'm...you could say I'm still swinging!"

They laughed over that. Sam Spry, in his enthusiasm, swaying in the doorway, his shirt swaying with him. But, suddenly, he turned his head toward me, smile vanishing, thick eyebrows lowering over dark eyes, "What the hell you looking at?"

Caught by surprise, I took a moment to respond, "I'm looking at you."

"Something peculiar about me?"

"Yeah," I hesitated for a second, took a chance. "Damn right there is."

"Hell you mean by that?"

"Well, man, you're not what usually opens the door."

He stared balefully for a couple of beats before leaning that massive head back, his mouth opening wide to show huge white teeth—so big they seemed scarcely human—and practically bellowed his laughter.

"Well, I hope not!" he finally exclaimed, adding: "Just testing you, kid."

He turned adroitly and we followed him inside. I was reminded, in spite of myself—I mean, I couldn't help be reminded

—of an orangutan but in place of jungle lianas, elevated rails led through the living room to the kitchen with tracks branching off to bedroom and bathroom.

In the kitchen at the back of the house, he let go his grip, dropping onto a couple of mats like you see in gymnasiums. "Have a seat, boys, while I get us something to drink."

The oak table was fastened to the floor with thick L-shaped metal braces. I watched Sam Spry go about his business, balancing on his knuckles when he had a way to go; from, for instance, shelves that rose no more than four feet off the floor to the apartment-size refrigerator. But when it was necessary to carry something, Sam rested his bottom on the floor, the load on his lap, and propelled himself using his arms as if they were ski poles, knuckles on the floor.

"Jimmy, this reprobate and me covered some ground, no kidding," Sam said. "Back when I had legs that was. We were in Spain together and before that did plenty of rough hustling across this country and down through Baja California. Ain't that right, partner?"

Floyd didn't deny it. Sam tossed him a bottle of rye; a bottle of bourbon arrived a second later, Floyd snatching them out of the air like a juggler. From the fridge, Sam brought a few Dr. Peppers and a half-filled half-gallon of Famiglia Cribari Zinfandel. This latter he didn't toss but held by the neck in one hand, laying the other flat on the tabletop and vaulting to his seat. Once we each had a drink, had wished each other a top o' the afternoon and swallowed, Floyd and Sam Spry sighed in unison, spoke as one, "Remember the time...."

And they were off, opening their battered grips and bringing forth all kinds of objects to be shared and remarked upon, held up to the light for consideration, to be admired or mocked good-naturedly.

As near as I could figure, these two characters had met in the late-Twenties; it had to have been before the Depression because they hoboed together and had no trouble finding work. They were what were known as boomer workers, part of a peripatetic work force, hopping freights in order to get from one job to the next.

They rolled along with their tales and I felt privileged to be there listening. Now and again one of them turned to me, "See Jimmy. We had to get out of that part of Nebraska because the farmer thought—he knew—there was hanky-panky going on, thought old Sam was cosying up to his daughter."

"Was he? Were you, Sam?"

"Hell, no. I wouldn't do any such thing."

"He's right," Floyd agreed. "It was the wife."

Sam actually blushed before saying, "Jimmy, our pal and me had to hide out in an old chicken coop on the next spread for three days while those squareheads searched for us."

"Forget the women folk. They wanted to string us up for a couple of Commies."

"Reds" Sam said. "What they called us in those days."

"You forgot the 'dirty.' Dirty Reds."

"Thought it was curtains when they came around with that hound dog. Remember?"

"God bless that stinking chicken coop. It saved our lives."

"Those peckerwoods had some big ugly guns, boy."

As a kid, Sam Spry had spent a few years working on the railroad but went seeking adventure not too long after high school. Floyd, around the same time, had shipped out, wound up in South America, participated in some coup or revolution, and came back dedicated to the rearrangement of American society in a more equitable manner. Sam was thinking along those same lines.

"Basically," Sam said. "What we were against was capitalism. If we'd been living under communism, we'd have been against that too."

Back then, Sam and Floyd spent winters in radical Chicago. They'd listen to speakers in Bughouse Square, attend lectures at Ben Reitman's hobo college, and had even met Emma Goldman.

They weren't old enough to have been around for the great days of the IWW but hadn't missed them by much. Plenty of

Wobblies were active in the late Twenties and early Thirties, many still fairly young men.

Myself, just two months previously, I'd spent time with some of these same Wobblies, very old men now, at a sort of rest home the IWW still maintained on South Halstead Street in Chicago. It was a great experience for me to hear those guys reminisce about the old labour battles. One toothless character said, "Bumming west are you? Well, I'll give you a tip. There's an old fellow with a spread, I'd reckon was twenty miles the other side of Cedar Rapids, he'll stand you to some grub and let you unroll your blanket in one of his haystacks. Used to pay him a visit every year up until the War."

He meant the First.

Sam and Floyd did not spend all those years at each other's side, far from it.

"You'd work the harvest in Iowa or pick apples in Washington State with your buddy then go your separate ways," Floyd explained. "Maybe to ship out or go logging. I even helped out in Carlo Tresca's printing shop in New York. Then, lo and behold, you'd run into each other at Bughouse Square or Biloxi or maybe a cantina in Ensenada. But more often, it'd be in some Hooverville or jungle somewhere."

Their conversation ranged over jobs of work and old radical heroes, time on picket lines, battles with yard bulls, scissorbills, cops and management thugs. They freely divested themselves of political opinions but never with the tendentiousness and stolidity, the complete absence of humour, that I was already familiar with, not only from old Commies their age but, worse, my contemporaries, who were just beginning to be called The New Left. Sam and Floyd weren't guys who'd put off having a good time until after the revolution. Their reminiscences, therefore, included bust ups and jackpots and uproarious nights with often a good deal of female companionship. Not that either of them bragged or even became graphic; no, it was all said in sort of joyful reference.

These were men who had lived. They'd grabbed life, embraced it, wrung its neck, kissed and fondled it, kicked it in the keister and held on tight. They'd taken some shots in return but didn't seem to hold any grudges.

And they were great yarn spinners. Floyd was the more articulate, being widely read, and he'd roamed over a greater field, nearly every corner of the globe, it turned out. Sam Spry was rougher, a volcanic talker and once he erupted, words poured forth to engulf everyone around him. At such times, he appeared such a powerful force—big mitts hammering the table to emphasize a point, huge head of thick tangled hair—that I had, on a couple of occasions when the booze had started to work, to actually stop myself from peeking under the table, half-convinced it had to be some sort of gaff.

It turned into a twelve hour session at that kitchen table and we were probably halfway along before Sam and Floyd got around to Spain. There had already been oblique references, more like asides, but the mood hadn't been right to expand on the subject. Later, I realized they'd been slipping up on it like a couple of Durutti's anarchist guerrillas to a foxhole full of Falangists.

Finally, they started in the middle of the whole thing, some encampment or earthworks fortification out on the Plains of Tereul, remembering days of desultory sniper fire followed by the sheer chaos of full-scale battle. They called forth comrades who'd fallen there and in other campaigns. Some had been naive idealists, not to be confused with certain others, professional ideaologues. Then Sam and Floyd went back to the beginning and, with my edification as an excuse, spoke of the Spanish Civil War as the last good and noble cause, certainly the last battle that could even remotely be called romantic. Talked about Franco returning from North Africa supported by the military, the Church, and the Nazi war machine, his intention being to overthrow the democratic government of Spain. All over the world the call had gone out for volunteers. In North America the word circulated at union meetings and lecture halls, made its way through city neighborhoods and went out on the road. Young men came from the slums and the universities, the farms and the hobo jungles.

Sam and Floyd got to Spain by different routes. Floyd heard the call while in some waterfront tavern in Norway, immediately abandoned ship and set out across Europe. Sam came over from the States with a group of radical-minded young men. Both had, of course, to slip over the Spanish border.

Floyd reached Perpignon with the name of a cafe owner who put him in touch with a goatherd who lead him over the border at night, and he made his own way to a meet with the anarchist representative. A few days later he was in Catalonia with the shock troops of the CNT.

Sam, arriving a couple of months later, enlisted with the International Brigades. "God, we tramped around in the Pyrenees for three days getting nowhere. One of those idiot Comrades had met us on the frontier and he immediately got lost."

"Leastaways, you got some training with the Brigades. We hardly did with the CNT."

"If you could call it training. Drilled with wooden rifles, marched round and round in the dust, a bunch of us yokels with some city slickers thrown in, all trying to stay in formation, all the time wondering if this would really help when we met the enemy. Must have been kind of funny for you, Floyd, getting the training after you'd already been in some fighting. Brazil or wherever it was."

"At least there wasn't much of it. Took less time than a hick town haircut. Later on what it reminded me of was all those pot-bellied scissorbills playing soldier when the Second World War was laid on us. You know, one-two-three-four all around the Armory floor—so as to protect Gary, Indiana from the Japanese."

"There were fellows from nearly everywhere," Sam said. "Lots of English and Americans, Canadians, but Danes too, French, plenty of Jews from everywhere and, of course, Russians."

"I still see a few of those boys here and there, one country or another."

"You used to keep in touch with Arvoldsen over there in Sweden."

"Had a visit with little Lars in Gottingen three, maybe four years ago."

"What the hell you doing there?"

"It's a long story, pardner. Anyway, little Lars is a big shot in television in Sweden but he's the same as always."

"Jimmy, that fellow," Sam said, "was the complete opposite of what we think a Swede is like. Know what I mean? How we think of them is as big blond bumpkins, sort of slow and with no sense of humour? But Lars, he was a dark, chubby sort of fellow and the shortest soldier in our ragtag army. Always cracking jokes and doing favours for people. First impression of him, you figure he must work behind the lines in a hospital but, no sirree, he was a hell of a fighter."

"About the bravest man I met over there. Says now that the Spanish war wasn't as rough as his television battles. Says there's more intrigue going on than in the Comintern."

Meanwhile, bottles were making the rounds, and every now and again one of these guys would pause after a sip and stare at a spot on the table, then raise his eyes and conjure forth some clerk from New York City, a Manitoba farmboy or Spanish university student who had been blown up, gunned down or gone missing in action.

Sam told about an old nun at a convent on the scorched plains who, in secret defiance of the Church—the priests reported anything that appeared to be suspicious activity among the local men—lighted candles for the Loyalists. Floyd saying some of his most vivid memories of that time were not of battles, bloodshed, escapes, clandestine operations or the brief appearances of famous people but, rather, of women and girls, not nuns either but ordinary women, bravely attempting to make do, to imitate normal life in the midst of the chaos. "In a little town near Madrid, terribly poor, there was an old fountain where the women gathered. We were passing through, trying to reach the gunfire that could be heard maybe three or four kilometres away. And by this fountain was an olive tree and from a branch there hung a cracked and tarnished mirror, and while the old women gossiped and did the wash, the girls gathered around this mirror. There was one lipstick thing and they took turns with it, painting their lips, then puckering them, studying themselves in the old cracked mirror."

The talk of women, of olive trees, lead to Dolores Ibarruri, La Pasionaria, and the defeat; her speech to the departing International Brigades. "Come back when the olive tree of freedom brings forth its fruit."

Remembering that speech, the day they heard it, October 29, 1938 in Barcelona, Sam and Floyd said that they had been in awe, remembered it in awe, not only because of the sadness and drama of it but also because they knew they were taking part in a special moment of history. Floyd saying that it was particularly poignant for him because he hadn't been part of the Brigades though he fought for two years and left some of his blood on the Spanish soil.

"'You can go proudly. You are history. You are legend...'"

Both of those tough men had to wipe away tears but certainly not the tears of old-timers crying over their lost youth. They were tears for Spain, for the freedom that had been trampled, for that last good cause.

"'And, when the olive tree of peace puts forth its leaves again, come back.'"

Well, naturally, more booze was required for replenishment, and the last thing I remember, still at the kitchen table, dawn was ruffling her skirts.

And the next thing I knew, I was waking on the floor of a screened porch just off the kitchen, bright sun in my eyes. There was a yard of sparse grass burned a pale, dead yellow. I had slept on a pile of bedspreads on a floor of yellow linoleum with faded green swirls of fern. There was the smell of the hot earth outside and the wood of unpainted shelves above my head. I wondered how Sam Spry reached the upper ones. In a corner was a railroad lantern, grey work gloves on top. I smelled bacon, and didn't seem to have a hangover.

Sam was at the stove, atop a wheeled contraption like a re-enforced tea trolley, cast iron skillet of pea meal bacon in his right hand, spatula in his left. Other chunks of bacon were laid out on newspaper on the draining board.

"Hah!" he cried, glancing over his shoulder. "You're up. And actually standing there without holding on to anything. I'll be damned!"

"The hell you think?"

At that instant Floyd walked in, hair wet from the shower. Sam looked at him and nodded in my direction. "Kid's all right. Merits our company."

He fried up a dozen eggs and heaped them on a platter, crisp around the edges, blinded yokes, and I've liked them that way ever since. Sam'd also sliced hunks of bread to toast under the oven broiler. It was a delicious breakfast complete with strong coffee made stronger by brandy.

We dallied over the meal, delaying our departure but, finally, had to leave. As Sam pivoted his rear end on the chair to lower himself to the floor, I noticed, and saw that Floyd noticed, the lower buttons of Sam's shirt were undone, revealing the mound of his white underwear and, on either side, like pockets in an old-fashioned pool table, a leather sack that was stuffed with ghastly white flesh. Sam grabbed one of the stumps of flesh, obscuring it with his big hand, and grimaced ever so briefly, "Goddamned phantom pains," he said, too matter of factly.

He bid us goodbye at the front door, hanging from those brass bars. When I waved the last time, he looked just as he had the afternoon before, a shirt in the doorway with head and hands.

Neither Floyd nor I spoke for several minutes until he mentioned we ought to be able to catch a freight north that afternoon. "We could pass through my old home town of Greeley, and maybe visit a lady friend of mine—bet she has a friend—outside Denver. Then in a couple of weeks there's the hobo convention in Iowa. Britt, Iowa. If you got eyes."

"Sounds good to me."

We covered another block or so in silence until Floyd shook his head, saying simply, "Good old Sam."

"I guess he stepped on a mine or something like that, huh? Over in Spain."

"No that's not what happened. Sam was in Spain for two years, saw more combat than I did, and he never got a scratch."

"Well, what..."

"Came back here to his old hometown, had to lie about where he'd been or he'd have been jailed for a communist. Got a job on the railroad. Sam was between a couple of boxcars, seeing to the couplings when it happened. Some negligent peckerwood son-of-a-bitch of a brakeman didn't do his job properly. Sam tried to leap free but he leaped too late."

I watched Floyd who frowned at his shoes as he walked. He didn't say anything for another block, then looked at me. "You should have seen Sam Spry in the old days. What a man."